My Camino

————⊶⚬⚬⊷————

A
Journey from Lost
to Found

————⊶⚬⚬⊷————

SUZANNE J. BRUSH

THE CAMINO

Copyright © 2021 Suzanne J. Brush

ISBN: 978-0-578-87162-2

This is a work of fiction. Names, characters, businesses, places, events, and incidents are either the products of the author's imagination or used in a fictitious manner. Any resemblance to actual persons, living or dead, or actual events is purely coincidental.

Printed in the United States of America.

Table of Contents

*"When there's a big disappointment, we don't know
if that's the end of the story. It may just be the
beginning of a great adventure."*

~Pema Chödrön

This is the story of a woman who loved deeply and honestly. She was hurt by those she trusted the most. She was able to forgive them, yet she struggled with forgiving herself. But, she believed. She had faith that "tomorrow is another day" and she believed in miracles. This is also the story of her great adventure on The Camino Frances.

Introduction

We are travelers on a cosmic journey, stardust, swirling
And dancing in the eddies and whirlpools of
infinity. Life is eternal. We have stopped for a moment
to encounter each other, to meet, to love, to share. This is
a precious moment. It is a little parenthesis in eternity.

~Paulo Coelho

Humpty Dumpty sat on a wall,
Humpty Dumpty had a great fall.
All the king's horses and all the king's men
Couldn't put Humpty together again.

For so many years I felt exactly like Humpty Dumpty, that egg that famously fell from his perch and broke wide open. I was shattered into thousands of tiny pieces, with no hope of ever finding all those I had given away or were taken from me. The ones that were forgotten and lost.

There were many years when I hoped that someone or something would put me together again. I have come to understand that only I can do that. I am all I have, and all I ever had. I'm not trying to blame anyone, nor do I intend to teach anything in these pages. Instead, I will share what I learned and how I learned it. I do expect to learn a great deal more, but I have faith that this new wisdom will come, not from a place of fear, but one of love.

This is the story of my five hundred-fifty mile pilgrimage along the Camino de Santiago, the famous network of ancient routes that lead to the Cathedral de Santiago de Compostela in the Galicia region of northern Spain. Of the seven main routes, the Camino Frances, or the French Way, is the most popular, walked by more than three hundred thousand people from around the globe each year. "Holy Years" always draw more pilgrims, including Pope Benedict in the last Holy Year, 2010. The next Holy Year is 2021, and the number of pilgrims will surely reach an all-time high.

I began my pilgrimage determined to make it a life-changing experience, though I didn't know what form that experience would take. Whatever else might happen, I hoped to shift certain beliefs that I was taught and had held me prisoner for such a long time.

For many years I was in an unhappy marriage. Whenever I've tried to describe it to others, I knew that certain questions occurred to them; it's almost as if I could see the words swirling through their minds. I know, because they're the same questions that have haunted me:

Why did I marry him?

Why did I stay with him?

How was any of that even possible?

My hope as I walked the Camino was to answer these questions, let go of the painful events of my past once and for all, and finally find my *true* soul group. I intended for each step to bring me closer to the woman I was born to be. It sounded simple, but if I've learned anything in this life it's that simple is not the same as easy.

Chapter One

Almost everyone goes through a time in their life when they are "brought to their knees." For each, the circumstances are different, and many people have faced far greater challenges than I. What brought me to my knees, and left me unable to make sense of the past several decades, was the cognitive dissonance I experienced during my marriage. My husband was an enigma, a "boy" I would never know, always saying one thing and doing another. He lied when it wasn't necessary. He was a real charmer, yet he showed no signs of compassion or empathy and was at a loss when it came to discerning "right" from "wrong." He was also incapable of intimacy with me.

I still think of him as my soulmate, but my definition of that word may not be what you expect. Most people think a soulmate is your perfect fit, your match made in heaven. For me, a soulmate is like a truth-telling mirror. It's the person who shows you what is holding you back in life, who forces you to recognize your own illusions.

Soulmates come into our lives to shake us up, tear apart our egos, show us our obstacles, break our hearts wide open and make us desperate to transform our lives. Can we live with our soulmate forever? Everyone must answer that for themselves. For me that answer was a resounding no. In fact, to remain with him would have meant my spiritual demise.

Total desperation finally led to divorce, and even then it was a very hard decision. My parents had divorced when I was in my late teens, and though it might have been years in the making it came as a great shock. To the outsider, my upbringing appeared close to perfect. Two bright, attractive and accomplished parents; an upper middle class, a "normal" family. When my mom decided to leave my dad for another man, the world as I knew it fell apart. My mother *insisted* on my support. My dad *needed* my love and understanding. And as my siblings were living in other cities, I felt like I was shouldering the entire burden myself. I felt I had to be everything to everyone.

By the time *I* filed for divorce, my youngest child had left for college. Yet I still felt I was breaking the vow I had made to myself so many years earlier – that I would never tear my family apart the way my family of origin had been torn from me. I had, somewhere along the way, decided that staying with my husband was my "cross to bear," that it was my job to heal him. This, along with my blind hope that he would miraculously "wake up," had led me to spend my entire adult life, up to that point, with him. For most of that time I struggled with depression and anxiety due to the confusion and chaos in which I lived.

Once the divorce was final I left the marital home and had another built for my children and me. It was lovely, and working with the builder and architect provided a much-needed distraction from the recent upheaval. I also started looking for a job. I was going to be on my own for the first time in years and I knew a job was what I needed in order to feel grounded in my new reality.

Fortunately, I had a friend, Chloe, who owned a chic boutique not far from my home. Her shop carried some of the finest and most stylish clothing in the Midwest. Chloe's motto was, "We dress our clients from head to toe." She understood that most women, no matter how much they appreciated pretty things, had no clue how to dress themselves. It was up to her to choose the clothing and accessories for them. Her clientele had money to spend, but they needed someone like Chloe to dress them!

I knew better than anyone how talented Chloe was, because I was one of her first clients. Now I was hoping she needed any help, and as luck would have it, she did.

One day during a lull at the shop, Chloe and I were discussing the books we were reading. We found we had similar tastes, including books on spiritual topics, but I was truly excited when she mentioned she had recently read Shirley MacLaine's *The*

Camino: A Journey of the Spirit. What had started out as a pleasant way to pass the time quickly turned into a deep philosophical discussion.

I eagerly told Chloe how much I'd wanted to walk the Camino ever since reading the book back in the '80s. Since then I'd read several other books by women who'd traversed the Camino as part of their spiritual journey. Though they each had different reasons for doing so they shared common beliefs, including the belief that each of us is here for a purpose. That purpose may differ among individuals, but on a collective level we had been placed on this earth plane to come into awareness that we are *all* sparks of the Divine. Finally, they all cited their walk on the Camino as a turning point in developing a more intimate and profound relationship with God.

"One thing she seems to believe," I said, turning back to Shirley Maclaine, "is that the Universe is basically good. I'm not sure if she uses the word 'God,' but somebody or something is in charge and He, She, or It has our best interests at heart."

Chloe nodded. "Yes, that's what she believes."

"You don't agree?"

"Well, I'd like to agree..." Then she said, "But some pretty bad things happen to people. If the Universe has such good intentions, why is that?"

It was certainly a difficult question, especially considering my own recent challenges. It brought to mind another book I had read recently, *Many Lives, Many Masters.* The author, prominent psychiatrist Brian Weiss, not only believed in reincarnation, he had made a career out of it. In 1980, Weiss "accidentally" regressed a patient to a past life during a hypnosis session. He didn't believe in reincarnation at the time, but later researched and confirmed what the patient had spoken

4

about through public records. Thus began his decades-long exploration into past lives, including the consequences of our actions from one life to the next – the phenomenon also known as karma.

"He seems to believe it," Chloe said, when I told her about the book, "But does he *really* believe it?"

"Well, I read an interview with him. The interviewer asked him that question very directly – 'Do you believe it or not?' And maybe his answer was kind of evasive, but it was still interesting. He said, 'The one thing I can say for sure is that past life regression is a really effective therapeutic technique. People believe it, and it helps them.'"

Chloe was still skeptical. "But does it help them because they believe it, or do they believe it *because* it helps them?"

It was the perfect opportunity to tell her about my favorite mantra: You'll see it *when* you believe it.

Chloe and I didn't answer the question of why bad things happen to good people, or why bad things happen at all. But there was no denying that we were impressed with the experiences Maclaine and Weiss had described in their books.

I shared with Chloe my deep desire to someday walk the Camino. Chloe shared the same desire, but while I, with my newfound freedom, could almost taste the experience, she had young children at home and would likely have to wait for years. We were each facing our own challenges, and we both felt that these challenges were not isolated or by chance, but part of a larger reality. I chose to believe that the "big plan" was essentially benevolent.

This belief was not based on religion, but my own intuition and spiritual beliefs. Nor had it been inherited by my family, who was mostly agnostic. I had always been the spiritual "black sheep" who believed in things like reincarnation and that our energy flows wherever we place our focus.

By the time I had this conversation with Chloe I had been divorced for two years. It had taken me a long time and many attempts at counseling before I decided to end the marriage, partly because I wanted to be able to tell my children that I had done everything I could to save it. When I finally realized his drinking and cheating would not end, I walked away. By then I had done an incredible amount of inner work, and I had reached the point where I refused to give my energy to anything I did not want. This had helped me let go of some of my self-limiting beliefs and begin the long and slow process of forgiving myself. I started to see these painful past experiences – and current challenges – as A.F.G.O.: Another Fucking Growth Opportunity!

Chapter Two

—◦◦◊◦◦—

In her book, Shirley MacLaine suggests that the Camino pilgrimage is a setting for all sorts of strange and wonderful things to happen. Some of those things might not seem wonderful at first, but they turn out to be wonderful because they're actually orchestrated by the spiritual power of the Universe, which is fundamentally benevolent.

My views on life are pretty much the same as Shirley's. Like her, I believe in the goodness of mankind and find the existence of evil difficult to understand. And *this* is what has gotten me into trouble. I could never seem to get my head around the fact that someone would intentionally do something to harm another living being. That someone would intentionally harm me.

In the years that followed I had continued to work on myself, reading spiritual and self-help books and seeking professional help when I needed to. However, things really begin to shift when a mutual friend introduces me to Lily, a life coach. Lily would become instrumental in helping me understand that I could be a <u>conscious participant in life rather than a powerless victim</u>. Over the course of several sessions, I come to realize that Lily is not only a gifted coach, but one of the kindest, smartest, most compassionate people I've ever met. I also come to consider her a friend, for whom I have a deep love and high regard.

Before accepting me as a client Lily gives me an extensive personality test. Admittedly I am a bit surprised when she informs me that, judging from my answers, I see life very different from *ninety-nine percent* of humanity! Lily explains that I am an idealist who believes people are basically good, kind-hearted and honest. The problem is that in relationships I often ignore the red flags, and my own intuition, because I want to make others fit with my idealized version of them.

Lily, and the tools she provides me, help me see there *are* people who see kindness and generosity as a weakness, who believe honesty and vulnerability are opportunities for exploitation. They see people like me as a means to their end. They use people like me to further their own agenda.

Realizing this is sad, but liberating. It is the beginning of a process whereby I would trade in my rose- colored glasses for a more authentic vision of life. Looking back, I understand that I was being prepared for radical, transformative change. I was being prepared for the Camino.

Around this time my mother has hip replacement surgery and I stay close by to help in her recovery. One day, she announces she's feeling well enough to venture out a store to retrieve some items she'd left for repair. Though it's a cold winter day, I'm more than happy to oblige. We've been spending entirely too much time cooped up in the house and are both in need of some fresh air. Little do I know how serendipitous our errand will turn out to be.

We no sooner walk into the store when I see Sophie, a woman I've known since childhood but have not seen in many years. Our parents were friends back then too, so it's a happy reunion for my mother as well as for us. After exchanging the usual pleasantries we fall into an easy conversation, and I'm amazed that it feels as if no time at all had passed. I don't know what makes me mention The Camino, but when I do Sophie lights up. She tells me she had walked it three years earlier.

I listen, completely enthralled, as she tells me about her experience. Not only does her account echo several others I've read – that it was a life-changer – she also provides a wealth of practical information. To make the trip as smooth as possible, she had hired a small company to arrange her lodgings along the way, ranging from small family-owned inns in the countryside to grand hotels in the few cities she traveled through. The company also transported her luggage from one place to the next, which meant she only had to carry a backpack on the road.

Listening to Sophie talk, I feel more than ready for my own spiritual pilgrimage. The Camino would be my way to uncover my destiny; it would provide that clarity to manifest the future I imagine for myself. I know it's now or never.

After that conversation I begin to plan in earnest. My first step, so to speak, is choosing to walk the Camino Frances route. I would start from St. Jean Pied de Port in the foothills of the French Pyrenees, and finish thirty-five days later at Praza do Obradoiro, the square in the center of Santiago de Compostelo, Spain.

Chapter Three

—◦◦◇◦◦—

Next, I book the same small travel service in Spain that had helped Sophie. I learn that the owners of the service – an American named Vivienne and a Brit named Kelly – had started the service five years earlier after they walked the Camino.

Vivienne had spent many of her childhood summers with her grandparents in a Spanish oceanside village. After graduating from college, she decided to relocate to Europe and for almost fifteen years has worked as a guide on the pilgrimage, leading dozens of groups along the Camino Frances, Camino del Norte and the Chemin Saint-Jacques in France. Her home is in Santiago de Compostela, right at the heart of the Camino.

For Kelly, the pilgrimage had marked a major turning point. She returned to England long enough to pack up her life, then she relocated to Spain, which she had fallen in love with.

I get to know Kelly very well through some lengthy video chat sessions. In between planning my trip, we share some personal details of our lives. It turns out that we have a lot in common.

Kelly is in the process of splitting up with a man she'd never married but with whom she shares children. Like my ex-husband, this man is not a "family man"; like my marriage, her relationship has been littered with red flags from the beginning that she chose not to see. Listening to her, I found myself transported to my own past.

As a teenager, I happily dated several different guys. I was having fun, and I liked them, but I never saw them as anything other than nice guys to hang out with. I believed they felt the same, but at some point each one asked me to consider "going steady" – the term for dating exclusively in those days.

As soon as they made these overtures I would end the relationship because it didn't seem fair to continue if I didn't see a future with them. Later, I would endlessly question why I had been able to call it quits with those nice young men but not with the one who would become my husband, despite the many warning signs.

I met Richard while standing in the quad with my parents, who had come for a visit. I was catching them up on my classes when all of a sudden I saw a young, good-looking man walking toward us.

"How are you doing?" he said to my parents, "Good to see you here!"

He then turned to me and with an outstretched hand introduced himself as Richard. I learned that the three had met previously at a special event on campus.

When he excused himself a few minutes later I didn't give him a second thought, but then we began bumping into each other around campus. He evenutally asked me out, and by the next semester we were dating exclusively...or so I thought.

I was young, naïve and pretty innocent, and he was insistent about having sex. After several months I finally gave in, but losing my virginity was still a big deal for me. I told myself that this was a milestone in our relationship, that we were on the same page.

We had our first sexual encounter on a Saturday night. The following Wednesday, he came to my room and said, "I need to talk to you about something. I'm not going to be able to see you this weekend because my girlfriend is coming up."

I felt like I had been punched in the stomach. "I thought *I* was your girlfriend!"

He acted like he hadn't even heard me. "Her name is Cathy. I dated her all last year and now she's working in the city."

"How could you have kept this from me all this time? You should have told me about her, and you *definitely* should have told me about her before last Saturday!"

I was hurt and furious. I felt duped because he knew I would never have had sex with him if I thought he was seeing someone else. Yet somehow, I heard myself tell him, "Fine. Your girlfriend's coming up, I'll stay out of your way."

I even tried to make light of it, saying I would "get a lot done that weekend." I wouldn't go out, I would attend to things that needed to be done. . . Who was I kidding? I would probably spend the weekend crying.

On Sunday night he came to see me. "She's gone."

"Good," I replied in what I thought was a show of strength, "But let's be clear that this will never happen again."

Things went back to normal, and whenever I thought about it over the next few months I would just push it to the back of my mind. Then he came to me in early May and said, "Cathy's coming up again."

"Okay, fine, Richard. But if she comes up and you see her, you're never going to see me again. You have to make a choice."

He had a couple of friends that were also my good friends, or so I thought. I talked with them about what was happening and they said that he was an idiot if he didn't choose me. As it turned out, Cathy did come up but he told her about me and as far as I know they didn't see each other. Still, as the saying goes, "A half-truth is a whole lie." The whole episode was an early example of what he could do, and would do, over and over.

I would also do the same thing over and over again. I would make excuses as to why I stayed. Later I would tell myself that I did it for the sake of the children, but what about in the beginning, when there were no children? Back then there was just plenty of warning signs that I chose to ignore. And what had made me stay with Richard, when it had been so easy for me to end those other casual relationships? Though it felt good to tell this story to Kelly, a person who had been through similar experiences, it still brought up more questions than answers.

Chapter Four

———◦◦◇◇◦◦———

Blessed is the influence of one true,
loving human soul on another."

~George Eliot

I go to Chicago almost every month, and when I'm there I usually meet my old college roommate, Evelyn, for dinner. I had known from that first day at school that we would be close friends, and we had remained so over the years, though our lives had taken very different paths. A VP for a large investment firm in Chicago, she spends much of her time travelling internationally. Now divorced ten years, I had become quite the globetrotter myself, visiting several countries as well as my children, who were scattered in New York and various other cities across the U.S. It was always great fun meeting up with Evelyn and swapping our adventures.

That night, over a delicious French meal, I tell her of my plan to walk the Camino, and that I'm going to fly to Madrid and spend a few days there before starting the actual pilgrimage. She tells me of all the cities she has visited around the world,

Madrid is her favorite; then, to my delight, she asks if I want some company on the flight. We decide we'll meet up in New York and fly out from there.

Six weeks and a flurry of travel preparations later, I arrive in New York. Eveylyn and I share a quick dinner, then I go back to my daughter's apartment and start desperately trying to "tweak" my luggage.

Packing for this trip had been no easy feat – first, because I've never been a light packer and, second, because of the climate. Kelly had told me that the only time of the year it's possible to walk the whole Camino – at least from the French Pyrenees to Santiago – is between late April and early June. Before that, snow and wind prevent travelers from getting through the mountains; by mid-June, the temperatures climb too high. My trip is planned for the last week of April, and the temperature over the eight weeks I'm there will likely range from below freezing to quite hot.

What's more, Kelly had told me I can only bring one large bag, as the van they use to transport their clients' luggage from one lodging to the next cannot accommodate more than that. After much debate, I had stuffed three Tumi bags, tagged them as "NYC," "Madrid" and "Camino" and hoped for the best.

Now my daughter takes one look and says, "Mom, there's no way you can take all of them!"

My son has joined us, and I stand there watching as they begin going through the bags, pulling out whatever they think is unnecessary. For each item they remove, I offer a perfectly good reason why I will need it, to which they respond with an incredulous look. An onlooker probably would have found the scene worthy of a sitcom. To me, on the eve of this adventure, it is no laughing matter.

Pointing to the tags on the luggage, I tell them I have it all planned out. I'll leave the bag labeled "NYC" with them. The bag marked "Madrid" will be used while Evelyn and I tour that city, then I'll send that one home with her, leaving me with one large bag for the Camino. Overall, I think I've planned pretty well, though I'm still concerned I won't have everything I need, not to mention the challenge of having to unpack and repack the bag at each lodging.

Chapter Five

Finally, the moment has arrived. I hug my kids goodbye and head off to JFK to meet Evelyn for our eight p.m. flight to Madrid. The flight is long – just a little over seven hours – and I'm glad we booked business class. Hopefully, I'll be able to get a few hours of sleep.

After takeoff we talk about my upcoming adventure and Evelyn announces she has absolutely no interest in the Camino. This doesn't come as a great surprise, as Evelyn has always been a more left-brain, pragamatic type. When I try to explain why I'm doing this, she is nodding politely, the way someone might when they don't understand the language you're speaking but can't be bothered to say anything.

I continue to share my thoughts anyway, though I'm possibly doing this more to solidify things in my own mind than explain it to her.

I tell her that there are as many reasons for walking the Camino as individuals walking it. For many, it presents an exhilarating physical challenge, like running a marathon; for others, it's a way to purge things they are struggling with emotionally. I'm mostly in the second group, though I see the physical challenge as part of the healing process. It's a matter of walking with the intention of gaining clarity and peace. There is one motivation shared by nearly everyone walking the Camino – especially those who choose to walk the entire route. They are committing to a spiritual search. To do this, you need to know what you're searching for, and what the search is going to involve. My search is for clarity, the next step in what I feel has been an "in between" stage of my life.

Although my marriage has been over for a good while, I'm still living with the experience of it every day. It is not bound by calendars or clocks; I can't say, "That was then and this is now." Yes, that was then. But "now" is not where I hoped I would be at this point in my life.

Evelyn, on other hand, is quite content. She is married to a wonderful man who loves and respects her; she has a son in graduate school and her big career in international banking.

So, to me, her lack of interest in the Camino makes perfect sense. She has made solid, sensible choices throughout her life, and she has already found what she was looking for. There's no reason for her to look anywhere else.

Evelyn knew all about my relationship with Richard; she had even been standing beside me and my parents when I met him on campus all those years ago. Now, that memory flashes through my mind, as vivid as if it had happened the day before. Why, I ask myself for the thousandth time, am I unable to rid myself of that years-long experience with him? Why, why, why?

When I bring up that fateful moment with Evelyn, the indifference she'd displayed about the Camino melts immediately away.

"Imagine it from his perspective," she says. "It was a big step for him to connect with your parents. Now he sees they have a beautiful daughter who's just entering the big new world of college. It's a homerun!"

Now I'm intrigued. "So what do you think was going on in his head?"

She looks at me as if I'm a baby chick that's just emerged from its eggshell.

"Are you kidding? He was thanking his lucky stars about getting a head start with you. There was no telling where that could lead."

21

Chapter Six

—◦◦◇◦◦—

Evelyn and I have only four days in Madrid together, and we plan to make the most of them. She has reserved rooms for us in a five-star hotel in the heart of the city – a perfect base from which we can explore. On the agenda are several private tours of museums and art galleries; meals at excellent restaurants; and shopping in the designer boutiques. Whatever we do, I intend to savor every moment.

The hotel is amazing, with a vast lobby of marble floors and columns reaching to the twenty-foot ceiling. There's also a man in a tuxedo playing a piano, but there are so many people milling around in the lobby that it's hard to hear the music.

Obviously something big is happening, and we ask about it at the registration desk.

"It's a wedding," a young woman tells us in heavily accented English. "I think the daughter of someone in the government is marrying a television star. Or is it the daughter of a television star marrying someone in government...?"

Whatever the case, Evelyn and I are too tired from our travels to think too much about it. We just want to relax and enjoy. There's a relatively quiet corner of the lobby with a cream-colored sofa large enough for a dozen people. We make a beeline for it, and a moment later, a young woman very much like the one at the front desk appears and we order two glasses of chablis.

"When I first visited Spain I was really young," Evelyn says, "The Franco dictatorship was just coming to an end. He was still alive, but it was just a matter of time. In those days, because of the dictatorship, it seemed like everybody wore a uniform of one kind or another. It was really noticeable. Then, the next time I came, Franco was gone and there were no more uniforms. The whole atmosphere of the country was completely different."

The wine arrives and we clink glasses to celebrate this memorable occasion. Talk turns to our plans for the following day, when Evelyn has arranged for a guide to drive us around the city and take us to a few stores. We speak excitedly about it for a few moments, then the exhaustion hits us like a wave. We sip the rest of our wine in silence, watching the throngs of people in the lobby, then head up to our rooms for some much-needed rest.

My room is large, very comfortable, and completely quiet – not easy to find in the center of a large city. I sigh, thinking this will be a great room for sleeping.

But as soon as I lay down, the Universe seems determined once again to trigger memories and associations I'd love to be done with. It happens wherever I am and whatever I'm doing, and I never know which event will emerge from the smorgasbord. Today, and for reasons I don't fully understand, the big wedding going on in the hotel brings me back to the day I moved in with Richard and Parker, his roommate. By then I was a couple of years out of college and working fulltime.

Richard was at work that morning when the moving van pulled into the driveway. I was talking to the movers when Parker walked out of the house. He looked confused.

"Hi Serena," he said, "What's going on?"

"Parker, my things arrived just a few moments ago!"

As I watched his expression turn from confusion to shock, it dawned on me that Richard had never told him I was coming. The humiliation I felt at having to explain the situation was palpable. Even worse, Parker was obviously displeased with the situation. We had become friends in our own right, but now, due to Richard's secrecy, our relationship had become very uncomfortable. I felt like I shouldn't be there and he probably felt the same way. Like all the "misunderstandings" that had occurred between Richard and I since we started dating, this was never talked through or worked out.

Richard had recently joined a country club, of which he was very proud. One evening shortly after I moved in, we had dinner in the club's dining room. It was just the two of us, which was unusual. As I said earlier, Richard was incapable of intimacy and because of this we never did anything or went anywhere alone. He insisted on always being surrounded with other people. But this particular evening, after drinking too much, he said, "I think we should get married."

Before I could respond, he added, "Let's get married on Tom's birthday. That would be good."

Tom was another one of Richard's friends.

I didn't understand. "I don't want to get married on Tom's birthday. How about if we have our own wedding date?"

We kind of kidded about it for a minute because I didn't think he was serious about getting married. He had been drinking too much, after all. Then talk turned to another topic and not another word was said about a wedding, during dinner or on the way home.

When we woke up in the morning I looked at Richard and asked, "Do you remember what you said last night?"

"Yeah, I said we should get married on Tom's birthday."

Suddenly, what had begun as a joke was going to be the rest of my life. It was surreal.

Richard agreed to move out of the house he shared with Parker. He did so reluctantly, but I thought it was important to find a place of our own. I found a lovely apartment not far from where we both worked and we moved in a month later. We set a wedding date for about nine months after that, and I began looking for venues, bands, and caterers back home, which was several hundred miles away. This was before the days of the internet, so it was not easy planning a wedding long distance while I was working full time, but things were coming together nicely.

It helped that I knew exactly what I wanted – a classic formal evening affair. I had been talking about my wedding day since I was a child; in fact, my father kidded me, saying I'd had every detail, save the groom, planned since I was ten. When we announced our engagement, Dad said, "I'll take care of everything. I want you to have whatever you want." He was that kind of father - always generous, always taking great pleasure in making me happy. He loved me unconditionally.

Chapter Seven

—◦◦◇◦◦—

One day I was flipping through a bridal magazine when I saw a gown so stunning it took my breath away. It had gauntlet-style sleeves made of silk and lace that ran from the shoulder to a V resting on the back of my hand. The back of the gown was a deep V from my neck to the waist and had about a hundred tiny, satin buttons. From the waist down to the eight-foot train, the V was inverted as it opened, in tiers, with intricate details of ivory silk and lace.

I tore the page out and took it to a bridal consultant. She discovered that the dress I'd found was made in Italy. There were none like it in the US. Did I want her to order it and have it shipped here? I said, "Yes! Of course!" and that was it. I never looked at or tried on another gown.

My bridal consultant had no experience with an Italian designer, but she was willing to learn. She took my measurements and ordered the dress in a European size that she hoped would fit. We both knew it would need to be altered, and boy we were right. The bottom was all lace, making it necessary to take the dress apart at the waist and remove fabric from the top of the skirt in order to shorten it. This had to be done several times, right up until the day before the wedding.

It was worth it. The magical feeling as I floated down the aisle, the train flowing behind me, was everything I had dreamed of. And Grace, my maid of honor, did an excellent job of spreading it out in all its grandeur as I stood beside my new husband at the altar and in front of the church. Even years later, whenever I looked back at the photos, the emotions would come flooding back and I'd remember how my dress had made me a princess for a day.

I also made nonconventional choices when it came to my bridal party. Grace wore a slate-grey silk skirt with a black cummerbund. The bridesmaids were wearing long-sleeved white silk blouses with grey silk skirts, also accompanied by a black cummerbund. They did not resemble any bridesmaids' dresses I had ever seen, and I loved their simplicity, an understated elegance to compliment the same neckline and sleeves of my dress.

The flowers were all very organic looking. None of those tight bouquets, just flowing greens carried in the crook of the elbow. Flowers lined the church, as well as everywhere the eye could see during the dinner reception. I'd had a lot of help on this front from my uncle, who was somewhat of a floral expert. He not only referred me to the perfect florist, but provided guidance that created the understated but elegant effect I was going for.

Now, as I lay in that bed in Madrid, I wonder if there will ever be a time when I will not be triggered into another game of "That was then, this is now… and this is also still then." I finally drift off to sleep, only to be awakened later that night by loudly celebrating wedding guests in the hotel corridor. I just hope for their sakes that the marriage is as perfect.

Chapter Eight

———◦◦◇◦◦———

After four relaxing days of shopping and sightseeing in Madrid, Evelyn heads back to Chicago. Though we've had a wonderful time, I'm excited for the next leg of my journey. Except for seeing it as a great emotional, physical, and spiritual transformation (isn't that enough?) I really have few specific expectations of the Camino. But whatever it brings, I am ready for it. In fact, I'm more than ready. I can't wait to get started.

As a parting gift, Evelyn has arranged for a car to pick me up at the hotel on Friday afternoon and bring me to the Madrid train station, where I will catch the train to Pamplona. As the driver pulls up to the building I am struck by the sheer enormity of it. Thankfully, I already have my tickets, but I have no idea where to go once I'm inside. When I ask him in my broken Spanish for directions, he just says to go down some steps and try to find someone to help me. Well, thanks!

Once inside I set down my heavy bag and look around, noting the many floors, all with tracks for trains traveling to and from points all over Europe. I head down the stairs as the driver had said, but have no idea where to go from there. Without speaking Spanish, how could I find anyone who could help me?

I look at my ticket (all in Spanish) and do my best to figure out what level, what track, and what time my train will arrive. Then I have to decipher what car and what seat I should be in. Somehow I manage to do it, then I'm off again, lugging the bag in what I hope is the direction of my platform. Thirty minutes later, I see the train pulling up and begin walking toward my assigned car.

That's when mayhem erupts. The train doors open, and crowds of people begin pouring out, even as others are wrangling to get on. I'm one of the last to make it, and as I climb the steps into the train car I look warily around. The area directly in front of me is filled with so many bags that there's no room for mine. Dozens of passengers are talking a mile a minute in Spanish.

I find my seat, but can't lift my bag into the rack above. Where is that gallant Spanish gentleman who's supposed to swoop in to help me? He's nowhere to be seen. I'm surprised by this. Whenever I have difficulty with my bags on a plane or in an airport, someone always comes to my rescue. Not so on this high-speed train, however, where it's clearly every man – and woman – for themselves!

Finally, I place my bag on the floor with everybody else's, then settle into my seat. Onward.

Chapter Nine

———◇◇◇◇◇———

The trip from Madrid to Pomplona takes about four hours
non-stop. I read through the packets of information I had
received from the travel service and review the schedule for the

following day, then try to shake off the chaos of the last hour and just enjoy the Spanish scenery as the train travels north.

Around seven in the evening we arrive in Pamplona, where I find the driver I had hired holding a cardboard sign with my name on it. The driver is British. He tells me he walked the Camino years ago and loved Spain so much that he moved to Pamplona. Now, in addition to his driving duties, he serves as a guide along some sections of the Camino and teaches at the local university.

The hotel is comfortable but very modest compared to the one in Madrid, which is what I expected. I'll be meeting the guides and the other three solo walkers the following afternoon. Meanwhile I get situated in my room and then head outside in hopes of finding dinner.

By now it's eight-thirty, but dinnertime in Spain is just beginning. I pull out my cell phone and open the compass app, which I always use when in foreign countries. I know I have to go southeast to get back to the hotel after dinner.

It's Friday and a beautiful spring night, so every bar and restaurant has a line outside. I walk and walk but can't find anywhere to grab a table for one.

After walking in circles for almost two hours, I go back to the hotel. There's a cafeteria attached to the lobby, and I wonder if I should have just settled for it in the first place. I find an empty table and wait, and wait some more. Eventually I walk to the bar and somehow manage to order a salad and a glass of wine. Kelly had assured me that I could get by without speaking Spanish during the Camino adventure, but I am beginning to doubt this. I had barely been able to get by in Madrid, so what will I do when walking through the small towns along the countryside? The optimist in me wants to believe that I will learn through immersion, just as I had learned French as an exchange student while in high school. During that year I had lived in a town northwest of Paris, and it was, linguistically speaking, a sink or swim situation.

When my salad arrives, I'm very surprised. I expected a simple green salad but this one is filled with tuna, artichokes, onions, white asparagus, red peppers, and other things I can't identify. Well, whatever. It's close to eleven p.m. and I'm not going to return the damn thing. I get another glass of wine and try to find a few leaves of lettuce to eat with the side of bread. When I need to get the check, I've become invisible again.

I try to flag down the waitresses, but to no avail. Finally, as midnight and the end of my rope approaches, I simply get up and leave. I reach the hotel lobby when I hear an urgent cry of, "Señora!" I turn around and there's the waitress, waving the check at me.

With the help of the woman at the front desk I explain to the waitress why I had left, then hand her my credit card. The end. I head to my room, hoping this night is not a sign of things to come.

Chapter Ten

———◦◦◇◦◦———

I'm awake by seven the following morning and head down-stairs to the hotel's breakfast buffet. In Spain breakfasts are always huge and this one is no different, but all I want is some juice, a couple of espressos, and a muffin. After I eat I start look-ing over some of my books and brochures about the Camino. I have always been very organized and like to educate myself before beginning anything new. This is especially true of travel, and before going to a new country I love delving into everything from its social structure to its educational and financial systems. For me, this is not only a passion, but the way I make myself comfortable. I have no fear as long as I have done my home-work! I become so engrossed in my reading that I don't even notice the passing time. The next thing I know it's eleven o'clock and the waitstaff is cleaning up the breakfast things. Time to get going.

Up in my room I get everything packed and bring my bags down to the lobby. They'll stay behind the front desk while I take to the streets to see Pamplona by daylight. The crowds and busyness of the night before has been replaced by a lovely, serene old city. As I walk I note some shops and landmarks, but I don't linger too much. Pamplona is a stop on the Camino and

I know I'll be back in a few days. Another hour flies by, and then I have to head back to the hotel to meet with my guides and fellow travelers.

I no sooner enter the lobby when I see a young woman approaching me.

"Serena?"

It's Vivienne, Kelly's partner at the travel service, along with another woman and a man, who she introduces as Stella and Adam. Adam, who was born and raised in Barcelona, has always loved nature and traveling, so guiding trips has become his profession. He has led wildlife safaris in East Africa, polar experiences around Laponia in Finland, and of course the historic Camino pilgrimage.

Stella is Canadian-born and, like Adam, is a world traveler. She lives in Santiago de Compostela, where she teaches English and yoga. Stella has walked the Camino Frances, Camino del Norte, the Camino Primitive, the Camino Fisterra-Muxia, and sections of the Camino Portugues. She has a passion for nature, culture, language, and movement, and loves sharing her yoga practice with others during their physical and spiritual pilgrimage.

Adam takes my bags and puts them into a van, which for reasons unknown to me they affectionately call "Brutis." As we're talking beside Brutis, two more solo walkers join us.

They could not be more different. The woman, Natalie, appears to be in her late forties or early fifties, and very confident. In heavily accented English, she tells us that she had grown up in Russia and came to the States for graduate school.

Standing beside her is Charles, an Australian man in his late sixties. Unlike Natalie, he seems quiet and soft- spoken.

A few minutes later, an athletic-looking woman somewhere in her fifties arrives, completely out of breath and sputtering about how horrible her trip from England to Pamplona had been. Her name is Charlotte, and apparently she had barely made her flight from London to Madrid, then missed her train. In a panic she had called Kelly, who helped her find a bus. It had taken her all night and several bus changes, but she has finally arrived, wide-eyed and frazzled but excited to meet with the group.

Once we're all introduced, Vivienne goes over some of what we can expect. Most of it involves their assistance with logistics, which is why I and the other travelers chose this service. It's comforting to know that the guides will be driving Brutis along the route, bringing our luggage to the next evening's lodgings and offering support if needed. Most importantly, they speak Spanish!

Starting in the French village of St. Jean Pied de Port, we will cross the Pyrenees into Spain, pass through the rolling hills of Navarra and the high plains of Castilla y Leon, and enter the magical province of Galicia before arriving at the legendary cathedral in Santiago de Compostela. As I listen, I think of the hundreds of thousands of pilgrims who have made this journey since the 8th century, all the lives that had been changed because of an unforgettable adventure. I can only hope it will be the same for me.

Chapter Eleven

———◦◦◇◇◦◦———

Our meeting over, we climb into the van and set out for St. Jean Pied de Port, France, about two hours away. Adam is driving, Vivienne is in the middle and Stella is to her right in the front seat. Natalie, Charles and I take the second seat, while Charlotte, exhausted from her night of travel, slides in the back and quickly falls asleep.

As we drive through beautiful northern Spain, Vivienne chats about her travel service, the Camino, and her life in general. She is very entertaining in an honest and engaging way, and I'm grateful to know she is there for support as I embark on the unknown.

When Vivienne isn't speaking, Natalie quickly steps in, confirming my first impression of her as well-educated, well-traveled, and very sure of herself. I keep quiet. Between the two of them, and the scenery flying by, there's more than enough to take in.

Finally, at around four p.m., we arrive in St. Jean Pied de Port. After checking into our hotel, we visit the official Pilgrims Office to pick up the various credentials that are provided through our affiliation with the travel service. Included is the scallop shell, a historic symbol of the Camino that every pilgrim hangs on their backpacks, and The Pilgrim's Passport, a booklet issued by the Camino authorities that certifies the genuine pilgrim status of the bearer. Like any passport, it's used to collect official stamps along the way and proves that each pilgrim has walked the "Camino Frances" beginning in St. Jean Pied de Port and ending in Santiago de Compostela. We will pass through many places that can't be accessed by car, and these stamps certify that we have actually walked the entire Camino.

The credentials are the modern equivalent of the safe-conduct letters carried by medieval pilgrims that allowed passage through the different kingdoms along the route, and granted them exemptions from tolls and other fees. Today, the document, which is printed and issued by the cathedral authorities in Santiago, is mainly intended for those traveling the Camino for religious or spiritual reasons, though it is issued to anyone who makes the pilgrimage on foot, by bicycle or horseback.

The Pilgrims Office is crowded, but since we're a small group we don't need to stand in line. By now it's after 4:30 and we're eager to get started on the pilgrimage. There has been rain earlier in the day, but the sun is coming back out and the temperature is perfect. Let's go!

Chapter Twelve

———◦◦◦◦———

L ike most solo walkers, I wanted my time on the Camino to
be one of self-reflection and spiritual discovery, away from
the distractions of every day life. So while I welcomed meeting
other people I'd vowed I would spend more than half of each
day to myself, and indeed there would be many days when I
walked alone from start to finish. Sometimes, though, I would
travel with another in my group for a bit, and that's what happens that first day, when I leave St. Jean with Charlotte.

Charlotte is athletic and very outgoing; she's also a bit of a
tomboy – she tells me she never wears makeup, and has brought
just enough clothes to wash at night and wear again the next
day. Charlotte also has what I think is an unusual occupation:
she works in a mortuary – or, rather, she works for a mortuary.
She and another employee, a man, drive in a hearse-like vehicle
to the site of someone's demise and transport the body back to
the mortuary.

Usually the death occurs in a hospital or a hospice care
facility, but often it happens in a private home. Charlotte is
eager to tell me all about this, and I get the idea that shock value
is one of the attractions of her job.

"Something I can't understand, and that really irks me," she says, "is when a three-hundred-pound man passes away in the back bedroom of a house, why the family can't move him closer to the front door when they know he's about to go? Does it never occur to them that someone like myself will have to move that dead weight out to the car? Plus, you're expected to keep a properly reverent expression on your face the whole time. Fortunately, I'm in excellent physical condition."

She then segues into her personal life. I learn that she has been divorced for over twenty years and has no children. Recently, she met a new guy and says it was love at first sight. As I listen to her story, I decide I find her really quite charming – she is honest, open and has a youthfulness almost bordering on naivete.

"But I don't mean to do all the talking," she says. "Tell me about you." Then, with a laugh, she adds, "Tell me everything!"

"Well, I'm also divorced, and when I hear what you said about love at first sight it brings back some memories. It was a very different situation, though. Lots of disappointment."

"Oh, was it love at first sight with your husband?"

When she says this, I giggle to myself. "No, nothing like that. But the wedding itself was a lovely affair. I've been thinking about that the last day or so."

"What was it like? Would you rather not talk about it?"

"No, I really do want to talk about it. I'd like to hear your opinion. Maybe that will help me make sense of it all. Because, from the time I left the reception and spent the entire wedding night alone, knowing my new husband preferred being with his buddies, I have never been able to understand just WHY he married me in the first place."

"What?!" Charlotte was incredulous.

"Yes," I relied, "That is exactly what I said. And how I felt… disappointed doesn't begin to describe it. The following day I had planned brunch for family and friends. When it came time for us to leave for the airport, Richard made it clear he wanted to stay with his friends, rather than join me on our honeymoon. I had to practically drag him away!

"So, did you manage to catch your flight on time?"

"Barely. At six p.m., I told him we were going to miss our plane if we didn't leave immediately. Again, I should have seen the writing on the wall…it was so clear! But my desire for what I wanted was stronger than all the red flags."

"I had dressed in a gorgeous tweed suit for our trip to Europe because I'd been told a woman dresses smartly when heading off on her honeymoon. When we arrived at the airport, several people in the terminal actually complimented me and told me how pretty I looked. As I thanked them, it was obvious that Richard was embarrassed or even somehow offended by these compliments. This would become his very predictable reaction over the years to any and all compliments I received. Each and every time he would say something so hurtful it took away any joy I felt at hearing the kind words. He just could not stand to have the light shined on me and not him.

"Anyway, it was a night flight, and once we got settled in the stewardess offered us champagne. I took out two silver goblets one of my bridesmaids had given us. She said that when she and her husband went on their honeymoon, they had toasted each other with a bottle of champagne and goblets like these, so I packed mine in my carry-on.

"Richard took one look and said, 'What are you doing?' When I told him we had received them as wedding gifts and suggested toasting our marriage with them, he looked almost disgusted. I remember his face was almost grey because he had been drinking almost nonstop for several days. He then shook his head, turned away from me, and fell into a drunken slumber."

"Did you tell him how hurt you were?"

"No. I was tired and heartbroken. The wedding was lovely, but I knew that this marriage was not getting off to a good start, to say the least!"

"But why didn't you say anything?" Charlotte asked. "I would have pushed him out of the plane!"

"That's a good question. Taking a stand right at the start of the marriage would have been a good idea. But I was too young, naive, and I just didn't have the self- confidence."

That first night in Germany we stayed in a beautiful old manor home that had been converted into a hotel. Beyond that we had made no reservations, because it was the "off-season" in Europe (back then there was actually an off-season!) so we weren't worried about finding accommodations. We just rented a car and set out with no itinerary. By mid-afternoon each day, we would find either a bed-and-breakfast or a small inn to spend the night.

"One day, about midway through the honeymoon, we were driving on a beautiful coastal road. It was getting late and I thought we should find a hotel, but Richard insisted I stop worrying. As day turned into night, I realized that he wanted to keep going in order to find a bar he had heard about.

"We did find the bar, but by that time it was very late and I was concerned that we had not yet found a place to spend the night. Richard began drinking immediately, and was drinking fast! Before I knew it, it was after midnight, I was exhausted, and Richard was drunk.

"Looking back, I should have just taken the keys to the car and left him there. But I didn't think like that at the time. I had no idea that I even had options! After my pleas to leave and locate a hotel nearby, he finally slurred, 'We'll get a room upstairs.' I didn't catch on right away. A room upstairs? It was a bar, and a real dive bar at that. But apparently there were rooms. It was then that I realized we were in a *whorehouse!*"

"How did you know that?"

"If you had been there, Charlotte, you would have realized it too. The rooms were filthy and had no bathrooms. Richard opened the door to one of the rooms and said, 'There's your bed,' then he left. I think I was traumatized by that time, but I was too damn tired to care. I just placed my coat on the little rumpled bed as 'protection' from God knows what and lay down, completely clothed.

"When I woke up the next morning Richard wasn't there. I walked down the hall to find a bathroom, which was disgusting. As I was leaving, an old, naked, and very drunk, man came stumbling out of one of the rooms. As soon as he saw me, he literally started to chase me. I ran back to the room – I was still fully dressed from the night before – and found Richard had finally returned to the room.

"I said to him, 'Do you have any idea what kind of place this is? I was just chased around by some naked wino! How could you have put me in this situation?! And where the hell were you all night?'

"He didn't answer me, or at least he didn't answer in a way that made any sense. By the time we got in the car I had become even more upset. I said, 'I've made a huge mistake. I should never have married you.'

"Then he started apologizing, saying, 'I'm sorry, you don't understand, you've got it all wrong,' but by that point I was too tired to listen and just sat there crying while he drove in silence. When we came to a decent inn, I insisted we stop and check in. After a much-needed hot shower, I took a long walk. It was a beautiful spot...lots of old ruins, ancient remains of some sort of castle from centuries ago. I walked alone through these ruins and I had to laugh at the irony. The crumbling ruins were like my dreams for my marriage."

I tell Charlotte that I knew then that this "marriage" was a sham. Yet, when we got back to the States I did not try to annul it, though that was the plan I made that day as I walked alone, tired and feeling very much lied to, "tricked" and betrayed.

And that night in the whorehouse was just the beginning. There would be many nights over the years when Richard didn't come home. When he did walk in the door, finding me hurt and angry, he would avoid eye contact, his way of letting me know there would be no discussion. If I persisted, he would extend his arm toward me, palm up, saying, "STOP." There was *never, ever* any resolution to these arguments, because in order for that to happen he would've had to tell me the truth. Richard had a saying – "Deny. Deny. Deny" – and practiced this until he perfected it!

Time and time again it happened, and time and time again I would let it go. It just seemed easier. The fussing and fuming weren't doing me any good, and it clearly wasn't bothering him. So I would push down my pain and try to start over once again.

"Toward the end of our honeymoon, we had a room in a small and secluded inn on the ocean. We went out to the beach and I said, 'Let's make love here. This is our honeymoon!'

Oh – and did I mention that there had been no sex at all up to this point?"

Charlotte's eyes widened in surprise, but she just let me speak.

"His response was, 'No, no...'

"I said, 'Richard, we're on this beautiful, secluded beach. Why don't you want to make love to me?'

"'And finally, reluctantly – probably because of my tears and begging – he did.'"

Chapter Thirteen

———◦◦◇◇◦◦———

"One of the most courageous decisions you'll ever make is to finally let go of what is hurting your heart and soul."

~Author Unknown

When I reach the checkpoint it's after seven p.m. I'm the first to finish, having pulled ahead of Charlotte for a bit. Due to our late start we had only walked five kilometers (roughly three miles) that day, but it felt great to get moving after that long drive through the mountains. The van is waiting, and when the others arrive we drive back to the hotel to freshen up. We'll meet up again for dinner at nine p.m.

In my room I quickly unpack and jot down a few notes in my journal. Journaling each day is part of the commitment I made to this journey.

By the time I shower and get downstairs the rest of the group is seated at the table with drinks in front of them. Some are on their second or third one.

Vivienne says a few words of welcome; then, although we've already spent quite a bit of time together, she asks each of us to tell the group why we're walking the Camino.

Charlotte is the first to speak. Although she didn't mention this when we were walking together, she says that her mother had died suddenly a year ago and left her and her siblings in deep grief. Charlotte is walking to honor her on the first anniversary of her death.

Charles speaks next. He is a man of few words, but seems to be a kind and honorable one. He tells us that he has a beautiful family, then says something about getting older and wanting to complete the Camino while he is still able.

Next is Natalie, who is just as energetic now as she was when she first met us that afternoon. For her, the Camino is a "walk of gratitude," and she refers to passages from several spiritual texts to explain what that is. She then urges us to ask her any questions we may have along the journey – not just about the Camino, but about whatever might cross our minds. Natalie clearly sees herself as a fount of all kinds of information.

Then it's my turn, and I find myself suddenly very emotional.

"I believe I'm at a crossroads in my life. I can see several different roads I could take, but I can't see far enough down those roads to know which one I should follow. I'm hoping that the Camino, which is a physical road, will help me find clarity while I'm at an all-encompassing crossroads."

I hesitate for a second, then decide to just go for it. What have I got to lose?

"In fact," I continue, "this is how I think of the Tao, which can be translated as 'the way,' just as the Camino can be translated as 'the road.' Here's a quote from Lao Tzu I have on my phone."

I take out my phone and begin to read:

"'The Tao can be infused into our nature and put to use without being exhausted. It is so deep and subtle like an abyss that is the origin of all things. It is complete and perfect as a wholeness that can round off the sharp edges; resolve confusion; harmonize with the glory; and act in unity with the lowliness. The Tao is profound and yet invisible. It exists in everywhere and anywhere. I do not know whose sun it is. It existed before heaven and earth."

As I finish speaking, I can feel a shift in the energy at the table. Is it because what I said is so different from everyone else? That's not what I intended, but something has changed.

There's a brief awkward moment, then Charlotte turns to me. "Serena, when we were walking today and you talked with me so frankly, I wasn't sure how to respond, so I didn't respond at all. But now I see how important that kind of communication is to you. I know it isn't easy to be so candid. I just want you to feel free to share what's on your mind and in your heart."

What a wonderful, reassuring thing for her to say! Then again, though I was deeply moved, the last thing I wanted was for the Camino experience to turn into an extended personal therapy session.

"Thank you so much," I said. "I'm sure there will be times I'll ask for advice or support from my fellow travelers. I'll also try not to wear out my welcome."

Immediately Natalie speaks up. Her voice isn't loud, but it sounds forceful because of her Russian accent. "No, no, Serena," she says, speaking my name in a way that suggests we've known each other for years instead of hours. "Don't speak about wearing out your welcome. On the contrary, all of us will welcome the chance to know you and to understand you, just as I'm sure you would like to know us. We must not hold ourselves back from each other on this journey. There may be times when we feel we should hold back, but if we do that we'll be very disappointed in ourselves later on. I assure you that I don't intend to hold back, and I won't stand for anyone else holding back either."

She says this with such overstated energy that everyone smiles. Natalie smiles too, but in a hesitant way, and I can see that she was trying to make an important point.

She and Charlotte were both right, of course, about what I wanted and needed from my companions on the Camino. But was it really something I could expect to receive?

Chapter Fourteen

—◦◦◇◦◦—

The group orders more drinks after dinner, but I'm tired and excuse myself from the table. Back in my room I get organized so I'll be ready with my bags downstairs by seven in the morning. Then I get into bed.

But it's Saturday night, and that's party night in Spain. The revelers outside are going from bar to bar, singing and laughing and having a great time. I'd like to keep my windows open because it's a very warm night and, like most inns in Europe, there's no air conditioning here. But even with the windows closed, it's at least three a.m. before I fall asleep. The strange thing is, I'm so excited about beginning this adventure that I quickly get out of bed and get downstairs by seven a.m. with my bag ready to go.

Each morning at breakfast we will have a group meeting to review what we accomplished the day before, and what we're looking forward to. This morning, we all agree that yesterday, our first day on the Camino, was a good warmup for what lies ahead. Everyone seems to feel the same excitement and commitment that I do. We're all ready to go.

Before leaving the States, I had done my research on everything I would possibly need on this pilgrimage. I purchased the correct hiking boots and shoes and anything else required for a thirty-five-day, five hundred-fifty-mile trek across Northern Spain. In the days that follow, I will be very grateful I had done so.

St. Jean Pied de Port has become the modern gateway to the Camino, the starting point for pilgrims from all over the world. After two nights in St. Jean, our group is ready for the trek to Roncesvalles, one of the most challenging ascents of the whole pilgrimage. It is also arguably the most beautiful, with those who make it to the top rewarded with a spectacular panoramic view of the Pyrenees.

We have chosen the thirty-two-kilometer "Route de Napoleon," so named because it was taken by the great French general to get his troops in and out of Spain during the Peninsular War. It was also favored by pilgrims anxious to avoid the bandits hiding in the trees surrounding a lower route.

Route de Napoleon should not be taken in the winter or whenever the weather is bad. That said, fog can roll in at any time of year, causing poor visibility, and that's exactly what happens this Saturday as we begin traversing the route.

The landscape is one of rolling hills and leafy green foliage on either side of the road and the farmland beyond. The single-lane road is well-paved, and now, in the early morning, nearly deserted, with just a car or van passing every twenty minutes or so. For some reason, all of them are going in the direction from which we've come, not in the direction we're going.

After the first quarter of an hour or so, our group has spread out so that we're each walking by ourselves. I am a fast walker and soon realize that I'm in the lead. The incline is very steep, and the trail so rugged that in some places I have to watch my every step. Still, walking by myself at a steady pace in this verdant countryside is a wonderful experience. I'm thinking about all the people who have followed this route before me. What brought them here, and what memories did they take away?

It is then, while I'm lost in deep thought, that Natalie appears beside me. She's breathing hard.

"Hello, Serena!" she says with a smile. "This is not a race, by the way. Are you in such a hurry to reach the end?"

"Hi, Natalie. No, I'm not in a hurry at all. In fact, I wish this walk could go on forever, if the country stays like this. So beautiful and peaceful, don't you think?"

"Oh, yes, yes," she says, still trying to catch her breath. "You know, Serena, I was serious last night about wanting to hear your story. I'm a psychiatrist, you know. Maybe I could say something helpful. In any case, I'm a good listener."

I hesitate as she gives me an expectant look.

"Well, I'm not sure..."

"Feel free to say anything you like," she says with a Gallic shrug. "Just tell me whatever comes into your head."

I think about this, and strangely enough an incident does occur to me. It's not something I recall speaking about with anyone else, but Natalie seems so interested and I don't see any reason to stay silent.

I start telling her about Steven, a friend of Richard's. Steven was very wealthy, and from my perspective his wealth made him feel he was entitled to whatever he wanted. I also sensed that Steven had never really liked me.

"What made you think that?" Natalie asks. Her voice has a note of challenge in it. Maybe this is how she tries to get her therapy clients to look more deeply at their assumptions.

"Well, maybe it wasn't only me he disliked. I don't think Steven had much respect for women in general. If that was true, I suppose he deserves credit for never getting married. He must have known he wouldn't make a very good husband."

Natalie is listening carefully while trying to keep up with my pace. "Please go on," she says, so I do, while at the same time slowing down a bit.

"As I said, I never thought Steven liked me much, but that all changed as soon as I moved in with Richard. In fact, whenever we socialized with Steven, which was quite often, he always managed to get me alone long enough to try to kiss me, or touch me, or suggest that he and I should get together later. If I told Richard about it he would just laugh. He never seemed upset that his friend wanted sex with his future wife!"

"And how did that make you feel?"

"Are you kidding?" I say sharply. "It made me angry! Richard didn't respect me enough to tell his friend to stop bothering me."

"All right," Natalie nods. "So what happened next?"

"A few weeks before we got married, Steven invited us to dinner at a very elegant restaurant. He had a new date with him, someone I had never met before. Steven always had a new girl – maybe nobody wanted to stick around once they got to know him, or maybe he was always looking for someone better. To Steven, the grass was always greener on the other side.

"We began the evening sitting outside, and Steven ordered a bottle of the very best champagne in celebration of our upcoming marriage. In fact, the four of us went through a couple of bottles on the patio before heading inside for dinner. Then Steven ordered special caviar from Russia, and with that, an overpriced Russian vodka."

"So you all got drunk."

"Well, the three of them did! I wasn't sober, but I was not as bad as the others."

I tell Natalie how after dinner we drove back to our home where we all skinny-dipped in the pool. After that I called it a night. I was exhausted. Too much alcohol and too much rich food and too much Steven. I said goodnight to everyone by the pool, and went up to our bedroom and collapsed into bed. After I was asleep for a while, I felt Richard get into bed. He rolled over close to me and began touching me. It was nice. For once I didn't have to ask him for this. I began to respond and we kissed. And it was a *good* kiss, very unlike Richard.

"Suddenly I realized, it wasn't Richard! It was Steven!"

"Ah," Natalie says. "Were you surprised?"

"I certainly was. I was shocked. I pushed him away and he just smiled. He was actually enjoying every moment of this. I told him to get out of the bed. I was furious. But he just looked at me with a mix of curiosity and confusion and said, 'Where do you think Richard is right now? WHAT do you think Richard is doing at this very moment?'

"He spelled it out for me. Richard was downstairs having sex with Steven's date!"

Then he very slowly got up and walked out of the room, leaving me devastated and horrified.

Chapter Fifteen

Remembering that night brings up strong feelings. I have been walking fast but now I stop and look intently at Natalie.

"Do you want to know what happened next? You won't believe it."

"Give me a chance," she replies. "We'll see whether I believe it or not." We start walking again.

"When I woke up the following morning, Richard was beside me. He must have returned to our bed long after Steven had left. He was sleeping soundly, as he always did. That always amazed me. Through all those years of pain, betrayal, and lies, he never had a problem sleeping. I, on the other hand, had more sleepless nights than not. Richard's behavior kept me awake and in a constant state of fight or flight, yet he never showed a moment of anxiety or guilt or regret. Or at least not enough to keep him from sleeping like a baby.

"I immediately woke Richard and asked what happened after I left the pool. He looked like he had no idea what I was talking about. So I told him exactly what occurred with Steven. He laughed at first, as he always did when I told him about Steven's exploits; then, as if a switch had been flipped, he completely changed. He got really angry and reached into his bedside table. Out came a large knife, which he repeatedly plunged into the mattress between us! He made a twelve-inch slice right down the middle of it."

I glanced at Natalie. "Can you believe it?"

She nods. "Yes, I do. It sounds like strange behavior – extreme behavior even – but of course I believe it."

"That happened just weeks before our wedding. Why did I go through with it? I was young. I was scared. I was in way over my head. When I look back, I feel sorry for that young girl. I was only twenty-three, and just a few years earlier I had gone through my own parents' very difficult divorce. While this was going on, I was given a message –sometimes subtly, sometimes not so much – that it was my job to support both of them. I was not allowed to be sad or afraid. Showing any negative feelings was looked down upon."

I tell her how I felt I had to be strong for my dad, who was heartbroken and confused that his wife of thirty years was leaving him for another man. And I tell her how I felt alone in this, because my siblings were living across the country. Everything seemed to fall on my shoulders.

As for my mother, there was no reasoning with her – no discussion. I was not even allowed to ask why she was leaving Dad, even though, as it turned out, she was leaving me as well. Eventually, she not only moved out of our home, but out of the state as well. I felt abandoned, lied to and, most of all, like I had no value or worth.

"One day I overheard her talking to her friend on the phone. She sounded so cold. She said, 'I won't let an old lady keep me from finally living with the love of my life.' She was referring to my grandmother – her own mother – who lived with us. Then she said, 'And I surely will not let an old dog stop me either.' She was talking about our family pet."

We walk in silence for a while. I sense that Natalie is thinking about how to respond to what I've told her.

"Serena," she says at last. "You asked me if I could believe what you've told me, and I said I do believe it. But now I have to make an adjustment to my belief. Because when I really think about it, there is part of the story that I actually don't believe. Or at least I have questions about it…"

"Okay. And what part is that?"

"I know a lot about men. That's just the truth. I know about men as friends, as therapy clients, and from intimate relationships. And I don't believe that a man would act as you've described without some reason for it. Of course, there are exceptions – mass murderers and so forth. But a normal man, or even a partly normal man, would not cut up a mattress with a knife."

Wow. Hearing Natalie talk like this is a shock. Is she telling me it was my fault? This is incredible! But it's not over.

With a sigh, Natalie says, "American women don't understand sex. Oh, I don't mean the mechanical part. They can do that. Babies are still being conceived in America, after all. But they don't understand how to satisfy a man. You see, Serena, when you satisfy a man he will have no need for sex with another woman. He certainly will have no need to cut a mattress."

Natalie is so passionate about this insight that she grabs my arm, stops walking, and looks intensely into my eyes.

"Do you know what is the key to satisfying a man? If you don't know, Serena, do you at least want to know?"

She waits for me to reply, but at this point I'm speechless. That doesn't seem to bother her.

"All right, I'll tell you. It's very simple. The key to satisfying a man is *flattery*."

Chapter Sixteen

―⸺◯◯◇◯◯⸺―

Now that she has revealed the key to a man's heart — flattery — Natalie suddenly needs a rest. I can understand that. Carrying around so much wisdom can be tiring. In any case, I feel like I need a break from her, so when she wants to sit down under a tree I politely tell her that I think I'll keep going. I don't want to lose my momentum.

My "therapy session" over, I can now devote my full attention to my surroundings. The countryside is still lovely, and to my American eyes it looks timeless, even ancient. There are no billboards or electric lines, and except for the occasional passing car it would be easy to believe I had walked into a different age.

There's a simple reason why northern Spain looks unspoiled: historically, no one has ever cared much about it. I wonder if maybe this is why it's become a center of spirituality, like the desert in the Bible. You can think about God because there's nothing to distract you. It's just a beautiful emptiness.

As midday approaches, I realize it's not much farther to Pamplona. The signs are hard to miss – the roads are increasingly busy, and with each step it seems the energy is shifting from tranquility to the hustle and bustle befitting a city of two hundred thousand. Still, it takes me by surprise. It's hard to believe that it's only been a few days since I took the train there from Madrid, but between meeting my fellow pilgrims and not getting much sleep, it feels more like a month.

Unlike typical tour guides, Stella and Adam are there more for mental and physical support than to recite facts about the places we visit. That's up to us. Having read up on every inch of the route, I already know that Pamplona is a place where travelers, pilgrims, and tourists have been coming for generations. Our guides do, however, warn us to be careful with our wallets, because petty theft has always been a problem here. In fact, medieval pilgrims were sometimes murdered for their sandals! "Trust in God but tether your camel" is a good piece of advice to remember in Pamplona.

The Camino passes through its heart, allowing pilgrims to soak up its rich history just by following the waymarked route. The cathedral and museum are popular places to visit. The streets are lively with lots of cafés and tapas bars along the way.

But Pamplona's worldwide reputation is built on the "running of the bulls," which takes place at the start of the San Fermín festival in July. Early in the morning on each of the festival's eight days, half a dozen bulls and nine steers are allowed to run through the streets from a corral to the bull ring where bullfights will take place in the afternoon. A typical run takes less than three minutes, but hundreds of people, mostly young men, come from all over the world to take part in the ritual. Hotel rooms are impossible to get during the festival, and the prices of everything go through the roof.

Since 1910, when record-keeping began, fifteen people have died during the running of the bulls. All of them were Spaniards, except for one young man from suburban Chicago who was gored in 1995. Without a doubt many of the deaths were alcohol-related, and drinking is now prohibited for participants. Good luck with that!

The bull-running events are now available for viewing on YouTube, and I suspect the majority of American viewers are rooting for the bulls. In recent years bullfighting has become controversial in Spain, partly because many people associate it with Francisco Franco's fascist regime that was in power from the late 1930s to the mid-1970s. On the other hand, it's also seen as a unique part of Spain's history and culture — and it's still a substantial tourist attraction.

Pamplona and the San Fermin festival got a big boost in *The Sun Also Rises*, Ernest Hemingway's 1923 novel. It's basically the story of a group of British and American tourists who get drunk and become jealous of one another during the festival. Although it's not the main part of the novel, one of its best features is the description of the same countryside I just walked through. Hemingway aficionados can visit the Paseo Ernest Hemingway, the walkway dedicated to the author, with a statue of him outside the bullring.

There is also an image of *Santiago Peregrinos* – "the pilgrims" – carved into the ancient stone pillar that stands sentinel over the magnificent medieval bridge that serves as the gateway to the city. Over the centuries, the carving has been seen by countless pilgrims, many of whom were making the pilgrimage despite severe obstacles of every kind. Now, as I cross the bridge, the carving reminds me that I, too, need to see beyond the distractions and keep my heart and mind fixed on my goal.

Those distractions will come in all sorts of forms. There can be bad weather. I could get sick or injured. There may be disagreements with my fellow travelers, and I already sense that being around Natalie may use up a lot of energy. These things, however, are on the physical plane, and what I'm doing now is a metaphysical experience.

It's been said that we aren't human beings on a spiritual journey, we are spiritual beings on a human journey. The world we experience depends on the world we're looking for. Right now I really believe that, and I want to continue living in that belief.

Chapter Seventeen

———◦◦◦◦◦———

Today's walk is a little more than twenty kilometers. Not very far, but by mid-afternoon the temperature has climbed into the eighties and the air is very dry. It has been a while since I went ahead of Natalie, and when I see her, reclining on a sofa in the hotel lobby, she doesn't look well at all. Apparently she had radically slowed her pace over the last five kilometers, and now she's feeling weak and complaining of a headache. Charlotte is at the end of the sofa, rubbing her feet.

"I think I became dehydrated," Natalie says.

"Well, you had a glass of wine at lunch," Charlotte points out. That probably didn't help."

"Oh, that wasn't it at all. I've been drinking a glass of wine with lunch my whole life. Like many European women, my mother began giving me a drop of wine at the dinner table even when I was a small child. In a very real sense, wine is the energy upon which the European nations run, just as cars run on petrol, although in the future cars will mostly run on electricity."

"But sometimes wine can also cause a headache," I suggest. Natalie brushes that comment aside.

"No, no, no. Wine never gives me a headache. And regarding dehydration, the very common cause is coffee, and I have not even had a sip of coffee all day. In fact, I rarely drink coffee unless it's that very thick and black Turkish coffee which is almost like a syrup. In any case, I haven't peed in quite a while, as one would expect when a woman is dehydrated. When at last I do pee, if I experience any pain it may be that I have a bladder infection, which can also cause a headache. The situation will become more clear when I pee."

Chapter Eighteen

—◦◦◇◦◦—

"Gratitude is not only the greatest of virtues,
but the parent of all others."

~Cicero

Once again, I feel like I've had enough of Natalie for a while. Fortunately, I have an excuse to make my exit: we're told our bags have been brought to the hotel and are in a storage room behind the registration desk. It only takes me a few minutes to sign in, get my key, and take my things up to my room on the second floor.

It would have been easy enough to climb the single flight of stairs, but after a day of walking I allow myself to take the tiny elevator.

My room is also tiny, just like those of most European hotels below the five-star level. In fact, almost everything in Europe is smaller than we're used to in America – lodgings, cars, even the people are smaller. But the room is perfectly comfortable, and after a hot bath I find I'm not even tired anymore. It's a perfect time to record the events of the day.

There is a small desk in the room, and I grab my journal and sit down. What happens next I can only describe as a true moment of inspiration. Nothing quite like it had ever happened to me before.

I start by writing a single word. Somehow I know the word is actually an acronym, but I don't know what the letters stand for.

Not yet.

The word is STARR.

From there, the words seem to write themselves. As my pen moves over the page I know I am discovering a tool that will be of much help in my recovery and healing from years of trauma. I was in an abusive marriage for too many years. I lived in denial for the first half of the relationship. I got through the last half by sheer determination to keep my family together.

I write, *STARR has five sequential points. SURRENDER is the point at the top of the STARR.*

I keep going.

I will Surrender to what is. I will not fight against my present reality. What we resist, persists. To surrender means to stop fighting a losing battle. Surrender is just the path of least resistance.

When I stop resisting and surrender to my situation just as it is, that's when things will begin to change. Resisting surrender is a shield I use to guard myself from pain. When I choose to surrender, I put down this shield and allow myself to be present in my life just as it is right now.

I don't pause or stop to think about what I have written. I just keep going.

TRUST is the second point in my STARR. It's

another difficult assignment, especially when we've lost trust in our-selves. I don't trust my ability to make healthy decisions. After all, didn't

I marry a man who "tricked" me for so many years? How stupid was I? How could I let this happen? Why didn't I stop it sooner?

I need to trust myself and my destiny. If I fall, I need to trust that God will either catch me or teach me to fly.

ACCEPTANCE is the third point of my STARR. Surrender, Trust, and Acceptance. None of these points will be easy when I'm in total despair and feeling hopeless.

But acceptance by itself isn't enough. I need to accept with gratitude. I have to accept the circumstances of my life with appreciation of my blessings instead of drowning in my anger, resentment, and bitterness for what I don't have.

RELEASE is the next point. That means no more beating myself up for any poor choices that got me to where I am today. If there's pain in my past, I have to let go of the past in order to get beyond the pain.

"I can't let my past define me. I am not my story! When I understand that, I'll be worthy of much more than the life I lived for most of my life. By cutting out the painful chapters of that story, I will reconnect with my authentic self – the person I was before all the anger, guilt and shame. I'm making a decision to treat myself the way I treat other people, and the way I want other people to treat me. I want to have some compassion for myself. I need to let myself off the hook.

The fifth point is RECEIVE, and it might be the most difficult. I really struggle with this one, but why does it seem so hard? Naturally, everyone wants to receive love, abundance, peace, health and happiness. But after living with trauma and pain that went on for years, opening my heart to a better life seems almost impossible. I actually do not remember what being loved feels like!

But I have to make the choice to try. As a young woman, I opened my heart to what I thought was love and truth. Now that I know it was all a lie, how can I find the courage to open my heart again? To be vulnerable again? But there really are no better options. I can't let myself be distrustful of life itself.

Taking the risk to receive is a risk. But not taking that risk is a dead end.

Chapter Nineteen

———◦◦◇◦◦———

Several days later, I am still somewhat awestruck by the inspiration, epiphany, or whatever it was that allowed me to create my STARR document. Even more surprising is that since then I seem to be attuned to receiving other inspirational messages. They have come to me almost every day, and all seem to confirm the principles in Lao Tzu's *Tao te Ching*, which is literally translated, *The Way*.

The Tao is the center, where there are no forces moving us out of balance. The Tao is not meant to be grabbed, or even touched. We simply "allow" it to come to us.

Now, every morning on the Camino, I look back on where I was yesterday, where I am now, and where I intend to be tomorrow. Am I still in the center of the road, or have I gone off the edge?

Going off the edge means losing balance. It means getting lost in one extreme or another. It also means seeing things "so clearly" that you can't imagine any other point of view.

As I walk the Camino, most of the time alone, I am always alert to the yellow arrows, the directions which keep me on the path. This way, I know almost immediately when I have gone "off course" and, most of the time, am able to correct fast enough so I do not go past the edge.

There are, however, three times when I go off the Camino. The first time I stop, waiting for the next pilgrim to come along who can redirect me. The second time, I find myself in a tiny village. I knew as I entered the isolated hamlet that, somehow, I must have taken a wrong turn somewhere. I ask an elderly couple who are tending their garden. They speak only Spanish and I still speak very little, yet I am able to understand their directions and find my way back to the Camino.

The third time, I go far off the edge – thirty kilometers, to be exact, alone and in treacherous terrain without the aid of technology. It's as if these three incidents, each increasingly dangerous and more demanding of my internal resources, are teaching me something about the greater journey.

The Tao, like my journey that day, is blind. We can never see where it is going. This is how I feel I have lived most of my life – slowly, carefully moving through a dark room, trying to find my way only to stray far from the center. I was walking like a blind person, but without the cane the blind use to locate the edges. I have gone past these edges – to the extremes – and this caused me great suffering. The Way is to FEEL the edge, but not GO there. STAY in The Way – Stay ON the Camino.

It is so perfect to say My Camino = The Way= The Tao= The Center/Balance.

Chapter Twenty

It's been a long day of walking from Estella to Los Arcos. The guidebooks describe this section of the Camino as "moderately challenging," but when you factor in the steady, cold rain that was falling the word "moderate" is not what comes to mind. Total mileage for the day was just 22 kilometers, but by the

end we were all tired and hungry. I am also beginning to wonder if I miss out on experiencing what the larger towns have to
offer because I'm so focused on reaching the milage goal for
each day.

It is evening by the time we arrive at the hotel in the small
city of Logroño. There is no dining room, so we ask Adam if
we can just order a pizza for dinner. He agrees and the pizza is
delivered – a rare similarity to life at home. Natalie, Charlotte
and I share the pie and, manage to have a pleasant conversation,
before the manager of the hotel – his name is Jorge – joins us.
Lucky for him, there's one slice of pizza left.

Jorge speaks English quite well and is very familiar with
the Camino. In fact, pilgrims on the route have been a steady
source of revenue for the hotel over the years.

"Yes, I've met all sorts of people, and the Camino is
getting more popular all the time. It's really a gift from God,"
Jorge says.

"And I suppose it's not exactly a wild bunch of people,"
Charlotte remarks, "Not a lot of drinking and so forth."

Jorge shrugs. "Well, people do like to enjoy themselves when
they're away from home. But you're right, they don't chase each
other around the lobby. Sometimes little things do happen,
though, and occasionally they're quite amusing."

At this point it's obvious that Jorge wants to tell some stories,
and I'm happy to give him encouragement. "Really? Like what?"

"Well," Jorge says, "most people don't know this, but if you
talk to anyone in the hotel business they'll tell you the same
thing. At least once every few months, a guest gets stuck in the
hall with no clothes on, or almost no clothes. As a rather small
hotel, we don't really provide room service, but if someone
wants something we will bring a tray up to the room. When

they're done with the tray, they put it out in the hall and that's when it happens."

"They're stuck out in the hall," Natalie says, "Fools!"

Jorge smiles. "It's understandable. Often they're people like yourselves and they're tired from walking the Camino all day. They decide to take a shower, but for some reason they decide to put the tray out in the hall after they're undressed, just after getting out of the shower. It just suddenly seems like a good time to put out the tray. Then the door closes behind them, and of course our modern doors lock automatically."

Yes, it's funny, and we all have a laugh about it. It's the kind of thing that you wouldn't think of unless you were in the hotel business, but it makes perfect sense. I'm sure there are things like that in every industry.

"So what happens when they're stuck in the hall?" Natalie asks.

"Well, it's not really that difficult," Jorge says, vaguely. "We can take care of the problem quickly and then we're all amused – including the person who got stuck, of course."

We chat for a little longer and then Charlotte excuses herself to go up to bed. I'm also very tired but am feeling that kind of manic energy that people sometimes have when they're exhausted. As much as I'd like to, I don't think I can sleep right now. Maybe Natalie feels the same way. In any case, both of us remain in the lobby with Jorge.

About twenty minutes after Charlotte's departure something shocking happens. It's the panicked cry of a woman's voice, and it's coming from the second floor. We all instantly know it's Charlotte, and we follow Jorge as he hurries toward the stairway beside the slow-moving elevator.

Charlotte is standing in the second floor hallway with only a small bath towel wrapped around her, looking terribly distraught. Could it be possible that she'd gotten trapped outside her room after we'd just been talking about that?

That seems a bit hard to believe, and in fact it's not exactly what has taken place. The door to Charlotte's room is partly open and a sort of muffled rushing sound can be heard from inside.

"Oh my God," Charlotte mutters, "I'm so embarrassed..."

As Natalie and I start to console her, Jorge brushes past us and hurries into the room. We hear him say something in rapid-fire Spanish, and a moment later there's sudden silence. The rushing sound, whatever it was, is gone now, and Jorge comes into the hallway looking almost as upset as Charlotte.

"Madame," he says to Charlotte coldly, "what in the world has happened here?"

But without giving her a chance to reply, he sprints back into the room, picks up the phone, and punches in a couple of numbers. When I look into the room, I see that a huge puddle of water has spread from the bathroom onto the carpet of the bedroom.

Two men from the housekeeping staff arrive, each of them carrying at least two dozen folded white towels. At Jorge's direction the men start using the towels to soak up the water on the floor, but there's a tremendous amount of it.

Then Jorge joins us. He doesn't speak, but just stares at Charlotte with an extremely exaggerated quizzical expression, as if to say, *What the hell happened here?*

Charlotte takes a deep breath. Her hair is wet and she obviously feels uncomfortable standing there with just a towel around her. But she says, "I got into the shower and took my clothes off. This is what I do every night to make washing clothes easier. I wash myself and the soap drains off me and onto the dirty clothes on the floor of the shower. But this time my clothes must have slipped down to cover the drain, so that's why it overflowed."

Charlotte describes this as if it's the most reasonable thing in the world. But does it really make sense? Jorge doesn't seem to think so.

"Didn't you see that the drain was blocked? Didn't you notice that the water was going onto the floor?"

Charlotte hesitates. "No," she says finally, "I guess I didn't notice. I think I was having some sort of spiritual experience. I was exhausted after walking all day, and the warm water must have made me very receptive to the vibrations of energy in the hotel. After all, it's not very far from the Camino itself."

This is as much explanation as Charlotte can provide. She stops and looks around.

"Now," she says, in a newly confident voice, "if those gentlemen can get out of my room I'd like to put something on besides this towel."

Chapter Twenty-One

———∞◇∞———

The following day, Saturday, Natalie and I decide to take a day off from walking. We're going to explore Logroño, do some shopping, and visit its famous winery.

I send my hiking clothes to our hotel's laundry and put on jeans and sandals, then we head into town. Natalie says she needs some new luggage, and Logroño seems to have more than its fair share of leather goods stores. Not all are created equal, however, and we pass several before coming to one that is clearly high-end. Natalie heads right in.

"One thing I really don't like," she says as she looks disapprovingly at a suitcase, "is dark-colored luggage, especially the brown Louis Vuitton. For one thing, everyone has it, so if you're walking around with a Louis Vuitton suitcase you're just another sheep. Also, if you're trying to find your luggage after a flight you won't be able to because there are so many at baggage claim, even if most of them are fakes. I want a large- or medium-sized suitcase in a light color so I can easily recognize it and so it isn't depressing."

As we look around the store, a young female salesperson is following us at a discreet distance, eager to answer any questions we might have. Outside the United States, I've noticed that women who work in retail are always young and attractive. Occasionally they're stunningly beautiful. This is obviously something employers demand and they don't hesitate to enforce it. I don't know what average-looking women do in Spain, but they're not working in expensive, tourist-oriented luggage stores.

Suddenly Natalie stops and turns back toward the salesperson. "Do you have any gold-colored suitcases? That's what I want."

"Well, I'm not sure we have anything in gold. But we might have something in yellow, like a lemon," says the young woman. She speaks perfect English with almost no trace of an accent, which is probably another prerequisite for employment.

She smiles and offers her a hand. "By the way, my name is Elsa."

We both shake her hand and introduce ourselves, then Elsa goes to see if there are any gold-colored suitcases in the back of the store. In a moment she returns and says, as if to highlight her familiarity with popular American expressions, "I have good news and bad news. The bad news is we don't have any gold-colored luggage. The good news is we have luggage in a sort of lemon color that is very bright and attractive. Would you like to see it?"

By now Natalie is bored with luggage, but she buys the two canary yellow suitcases Elsa brings out on the condition that they be immediately delivered to our hotel.

Elsa hesitates, probably because the store doesn't usually provide delivery, then says, "Yes, I'm sure I can find someone who can do that."

Back on the street, Natalie says, "I'm grumpy now."

"Really? Why?"

"I don't know."

We start walking, and soon discover something quite unexpected – a Sephora, and one equal to any in Beverly Hills or New York. Two young saleswomen, also very attractive, approach us and start talking about makeup ideas. In a moment both Natalie and I are getting full-fledged makeovers.

When the makeovers are finished, we both look like entirely different people. Natalie smiles, leans toward me, and whispers, "I am no longer grumpy."

When the saleswomen suggestively ask if we'd like to take the various cosmetics with us, I politely decline but Natalie goes for it, again on the condition that the purchase can be delivered to the hotel.

"I don't want to be carrying around a shopping bag all day," she says.

When she's assured that delivery can be taken care of, Natalie pays for her purchases and we decide to get something to eat in the little patio restaurant that the store provides.

Natalie says, "You may wonder why I speak English to these salesgirls when I could just as easily speak Spanish. It's because they're flattered when I speak English to them. They're girls from the countryside – in the past they would have been called peasant girls – and they've studied hard to learn English. So when I speak English with them they feel like I'm their equal. That's why I do it."

It's obvious that after the makeover Natalie is feeling very good about herself. Just for fun, I decide to flatter her and see how much of it she can take.

As we nibble on some cheese and bread, I say, "I really admire your ability with languages, Natalie, especially since my Spanish is pretty much just 'hello,' 'thank you,' and 'goodbye.' How many languages do you actually speak?"

"Besides Spanish and French," she replies, "I also know some Italian and a little Romanian. Plus Russian, of course. But many words and phrases in Russian are simply untranslatable. 'Yolke polke,' for example. Literally it means wood and Christmas trees, but it's really an expression of exasperation or impatience. Perhaps the closest English approximation is 'fiddlesticks.'"

"Fascinating."

"Yes, languages are fascinating. The various nuances of meaning."

We split the bill for the cheeses and continue our day of sightseeing and shopping. But I'm also hoping for something more substantial from Natalie. I do respect her as an intelligent woman, albeit an extremely egotistical one, and I'm especially interested in her as a professional psychotherapist.

Chapter Twenty-Two

—◦◦◇◇◦◦—

As we walk along, I feel like I want to share with Natalie the STARR revelation that came to me the other night – first, because I sincerely want to get her opinion, and second, because I'm tired of how she has managed to dominate every conversation since our group set out on the Camino.

Immediately, I feel the same rush of excitement as when I first thought of it. After briefly mentioning what a pivotal moment this had been for me, I get into the first point.

"The S stands for surrender," I begin. "Surrender is very different from defeat, because defeat is imposed from outside but surrender is an internal choice. You don't have to be losing in order to surrender. You just choose to make changes in what you've been doing and start off in another direction."

I glance over at Natalie and am glad to see that she seems to be listening intently.

"Trust is the second point," I continue. We often think of trust in terms of our relationship to other people. We either find someone trustworthy or not deserving of our trust. Just like surrender, trust is also an internal process. We need to trust ourselves. For instance, I need to trust my ability to overcome the trauma of a destructive marriage that went on for many years. I need to trust the decisions I've made when I finally—"

Just then Natalie speaks up. "Serena, I'm sorry to interrupt, but when you talk like this you're implicitly asking me to put aside many years of professional training. That's very difficult for me to do. In fact, doing so would even be irresponsible because I would be passively listening to you go on and on without informing you of the real science behind the issues you're talking about."

Before I can say a word, Natalie is off and running. She's talking very fast. She's even walking faster than before. I'm tempted to just let her go on ahead. Would she even notice that I'm not beside her anymore?

"To understand the experience of trauma, especially emotional trauma, you need to have some understanding of how the brain actually works. You're familiar with the right brain/left brain concept? Most people have heard about that. In a normal brain, a traumatic experience is initially received in the left side of the brain and often there's an immediate physical reaction, like screaming or throwing a coffee cup against the wall. Then the left brain transfers the experience to the right brain, where the trauma is processed and eventually assimilated so that it loses its power. Do you understand this so far?"

As usual, Natalie doesn't wait for me to reply. She just plows right on ahead.

"However, when trauma has continued over a long period of time, the transmission mechanism from the left side to the right side of the brain can't do its job. The trauma stays stuck on the left side and continues to express itself physically. Eventually there can even be chronic diseases like lupus or something."

Although I already know about trauma and how it does, indeed, get "stuck" in a part of the brain, I don't want Natalie to slow down. So I say, "Natalie, this sounds very important and interesting. I'm eager for more details. When you say the trauma stays stuck on the left side, what form does the trauma take?"

I should have expected Natalie to be irritated by any questions from me, and that's exactly what happens.

"Serena," she says, "I've tried my best to explain these neurobiological processes in a way that would be understandable to a layman like yourself. There's really no point in my going into more detail. If I were to do that, it just wouldn't make sense to you. I might as well be speaking Chinese."

Uh huh... I think to myself, *How very thoughtful of you, Natalie!*

Chapter Twenty-Three

———◦◇◇◇◦———

Later in the afternoon we visit the gorgeous winery, which is fun and educational.

Not long after the Guggenheim Museum in Bilbao was finished in 1997, the owners of the Marques de Riscal winery invited Frank Gehry, the museum's architect, to visit their vineyard, which is sixty miles south of Bilbao.

The plan was to coax Gehry into designing a winery on the property. Gehry was reluctant to design a small building and one so close to the Guggenheim, but he quickly recognized an ideal location for a hotel. It was on a rise with views of the vineyards, and also of the medieval town of Elciego, with its sixteenth-century church. A bottle of Rioja from 1929, the year of Gehry's birth, closed the deal.

Most everyone walking the Camino wants to see the Riscal winery, and most everyone is surprised that Frank Gehry did *not* design it. But the hotel he designed is next door, with the two separate buildings connected by a glass-enclosed walkway. We decide not to see the inside of the hotel, but we do take a tour of the winery. Afterwards, we head to the little café area and enjoy some excellent red and white wines.

I want to let Natalie know that I was not especially pleased, and possibly somewhat offended, by her lecturing me when I tried to tell her about STARR. But, in the spirit of our spiritual pilgrimage, I decide to let it go.

Instead, I say, "Natalie, hearing about how the brain processes trauma isn't especially helpful to someone who's trying to recover from trauma in their everyday life. If you're stuck in a traffic jam that's preventing you from getting where you need to go, it's not very useful to hear about how a car engine works. Do you see what I mean?"

Natalie nods thoughtfully. She's able to recognize when she's gone too far.

"I see what you mean," she says. "Well, let's try something different. Why don't you tell me about a specific experience you had, and I'll try to respond in a helpful way?"

"That's a good idea," I reply, thinking that I've certainly got enough stories like that. Just like that one in particular pops into mind and, perhaps aided by the wine, I eagerly launch into it.

We had been married for less than a year when I attempted to have a discussion with Richard about having a baby. I told him how much I was looking forward to starting our family. I expressed my deep desire to become a mother. His reply: "Fine, get off birth control."

This was *not* how I thought this conversation would go. I had been taking the birth control pill up until now, but I wasn't asking his *permission* to get pregnant! In hindsight, we never had real, adult conversations when it came to *us*. We both should have been discussing a family long before that point. I thought I was encouraging him to have an honest and heartfelt conversation about when WE would begin our family, but once again my hopes and expectations seemed too much to ask for. I know now that I had no idea exactly WHO that man was, the one I had married.

I pause for a moment, anticipating an interruption from Natalie, but she is just listening intently.

"That was in early autumn," I continue, "By spring, Richard and I were planning a trip to the Caribbean. By the time we arrived on the island, I was not feeling well. Something was definitely "wrong." I had no desire to drink the delicious rum drinks offered to us at every turn; nor did I want to sunbathe or even sit in a hot tub. I only wanted to eat the fresh fruit and sleep. I had no previous experience, but I suspected I must be pregnant. I tried to find a home pregnancy test but there were none to be found. It wouldn't be easy, but I'd just have to wait until we got home."

As soon as we returned to the States, I made an appointment with my doctor, which coincidentally fell during a visit from Debbie, another college pal. That day, Debbie went shopping while I waited anxiously for the results of the blood test. When my doctor announced that I was indeed pregnant, I was thrilled! Afterwards, I met up with Debbie and shared the wonderful news. I also told her how excited I was to tell Richard that he was going to be a father that evening.

When Richard arrived home, I asked him for a moment alone in our bedroom. I said, "I've got something to tell you. I'm pregnant. We're going to have a baby! You are going to be a father!"

I had a vision of how my husband would respond to that news, but my vision was not what I got. Richard looked at me, went totally pale, and said, "Oh shit. This means I've really got to grow up." Then he walked out of the bedroom and in the direction of the den.

I started to follow but stopped when I saw Debbie in the kitchen. Confused and hurt, I blurted out what had just happened.

She didn't offer much in the way of support or comfort, and when a few minutes later Richard came out of the study and said, "Hey, Debbie, want to go out drinking?" she replied, "Sure!"

I love my friend, but she's always been unpredictable. I cannot say I was shocked by her response. Hurt and betrayed, yes, but not shocked.

At this point, Natalie's eyes widen, but again she remains silent and lets me continue.

"Off they went, both knowing I wouldn't go with them – *BECAUSE I WAS PREGNANT!* The last thing I wanted was to sit in a bar with them, stone-cold sober, while they got drunk. In fact, I didn't want to be anywhere near my husband after his response to learning he was to become a parent for the first time."

A few days later I started to bleed. Terrified, I saw my doctor, who suspected I was indeed miscarrying. She instructed me to go home and get into bed. I was to call her as soon as I passed the embryonic sac. (Back then, ultrasounds, which would have provided much more information, were unusual.) I went home, crawled into bed and stayed there for nearly two weeks. The doctor's office kept in regular contact, and when the bleeding finally came to a stop, they told me to come in.

I walked into the office that day with a heavy heart and prepared for the worst. Instead, while doing the ultrasound, the doctor matter-of-factly announced that the baby was alive! Thank God! Again, I had no frame of reference for any of this, and it didn't help that my doctor had clearly missed the bedside manner class in med school!

Meanwhile, Richard went to the office each day and never showed any concern. I had spent two weeks in bed, pregnant for the first time, afraid I was losing my baby. I had no family near me, since moving across the country to be with Richard, and precious few real friends there. So I clung to the hope that Richard would do exactly what he told me he *had* to do now – *GROW UP!* All this hope did, though, was blind me to the truth: that our so-called marriage would not only not improve, but deteriorate more and more with each passing year.

"When I was in my seventh or eighth month we joined a group of our friends for a pool party. As I sat on the edge with my legs dangling in the water, the new wife of one of Richard's friends approached.

"'You must be so excited!'" she exclaimed. 'I just know that Richard is going to be the best father.'

"*Wow,* I remember thinking, *and how do you know this?* Worse, I had an awful feeling that Richard had absolutely no clue HOW to be a father, especially since up to this point he had proven that he had no desire to be my husband. What was I thinking?"

Even as I say those words to Natalie, I realize I know exactly what I was thinking back then. I wanted so badly to believe I was married to a guy who honored his wedding vows. I needed to believe that he *wanted* to create this family. I refused to allow the truth of what he DID, and what I SAW, to become real. I held onto my hope that when the baby arrived he would become a better husband, and ultimately, an acceptable father.

"Perhaps it was just a matter of selfishness," I muse, more to myself than to Natalie. "I wanted so badly to have children and create a loving and close family. After my mother left, after our family imploded, I felt this powerful need to build a family of my own. And I was never going to allow anything to damage it!

I could have succeeded at this, had I chosen a different partner. Shame on me!

"After that I went on to have several children and suffered as many miscarriages as live births. About ten years into the marriage, my mother came for a visit. We were sitting at the kitchen table and she asked me, 'Why? Why do you want another child with that man?'

"I said, 'Because I still have hope. I hope he will change.'"

Finally finished, I sit back in my chair and eagerly await Natalie's response. Just then I realize that a gentleman has approached our table and is waiting to speak with us.

Puzzled, I look up at him. "Can we help you?"

"Please excuse me," he says with a smile. "I don't mean to interrupt you but…"

He is obviously an American, and probably walking the Camino just like us. He looks to be in his forties or early fifties and is in good shape but not really athletic. He's wearing a white cotton shirt and white denim pants, with a white bandana loosely knotted around his neck. It's an American tourist's idea of how the owner of a Spanish estate might dress on a casual weekend, which ironically only makes him seem all the more American. He's not bald, but his hair is definitely thinning in the front.

"There's something I just have to ask you," he says, looking directly at me, "Where did you go to school?"

It's a mundane question, but I'm rather taken aback because he says it like it's the most exciting thing in the world.

"School?" I ask, "Do you mean college?"

"College, please."

I tell him where I went and he nods, still smiling, but I can see he's disappointed. "Yes, I'm familiar with that university.

But I could have sworn I remember you from *my* college. I don't think we ever actually met, but I remember seeing you on campus. Or somebody with an uncanny resemblance to you."

"How fascinating," Natalie says indifferently.

I can see he wants me to ask where, in fact, he went to college, so I play along.

"Oh, I'm a Harvard man through and through," he replies with a self-deprecating tone that is not quite convincing. "I lived in Dunster House as an undergrad, then did a joint MBA/JD program. Well, I've really enjoyed meeting you both and, again, I apologize for the interruption. Have a great day."

He turns away, then looks back. "By the way, my name is Nate. And you are…?"

I notice he's looking only at me, as if Natalie were not even sitting at the table. It's as if he's intentionally ignoring her.

"I'm Serena," I answer with a smile.

"Ah, Serena," he repeats. "Well, have a delightful afternoon."

And then he's gone.

Chapter Twenty-Four

———◦◦◊◦◦———

It's late in the afternoon when Natalie and I return to the hotel, both of us a bit tired from the full day. Was it an enjoyable day? In some ways yes and in some ways no. Natalie is a challenging travel companion, but she's also an interesting one. Her behavior is becoming more predictable to me as each day passes. When I bring something up, I have an idea of how she'll respond but I'm never exactly sure. She will always have an answer, but I don't know if that answer is fact or something she invents in order to sound knowledgeable.

We meet Charlotte and Stella in the lobby. On the Camino all day, they of course have walked much more than we did, yet they don't seem at all fatigued. In fact, Charlotte exhibits a level of energy seemingly designed to shame Natalie and me for not walking every inch of the route. I know she's proud of her identity as an athlete, but this is over the top!

Incredibly enough, Stella suggests a yoga session – "For just an hour or so" – on the lawn before dinner. She even invites a few random female hotel guests who happen to be in the lobby.

Even more surprising, Natalie seems eager to do it.

"That's an excellent idea," she says, "especially before dinner. That way our metabolism will be energized for digestion, whereas if we did yoga after dinner we would probably feel bloated, depending on what we eat, of course."

I don't feel like doing yoga, but I decide to go along with the others rather than looking like a party pooper. A few minutes later, with everyone changed into their own versions of yoga attire, we're on the lawn and ready to go.

Fortunately, it's a lovely warm evening.

There are six women in all, plus Stella. I make sure I'm in the back of the group. Though not an expert I do have some experience with yoga, and I can tell that Stella is an excellent instructor who takes an interest in each participant. At the end of the session, as we're all heading back toward the entrance to the hotel, I notice her coming toward me.

Oh no! I'm pretty sure Stella's going to comment on my work in class, and absolutely sure Natalie won't be at all happy. She had been to my left during the hour-long class, and after drinking all afternoon she wasn't exactly steady on her feet, or any other pose for that matter.

"Serena, how long have you been practicing yoga?" Stella asks me.

"Oh, not that long," I say as I continue walking toward the hotel as if in a hurry. But then I make the mistake of thanking her for teaching the class, and she says something about how good my form was. Natalie is standing right there and Stella is complimenting *me*, not *her!* I mutter another thank you and rush off to my room.

Chapter Twenty-Five

When I come down for dinner Natalie makes a show of announcing there's no room for me at her table.

"Oh, Serena, I just don't know *where* you'll find a seat."

She's right. The restaurant is a small, bistro-style place. Everyone in the hotel seems to be eating there at the same time. All the tables are full.

Just then I feel someone gently touch my arm. I look around and see that it's Nate, the guy we'd met at the winery.

"Would you please join us?" he says, already motioning for a waiter to bring an extra chair. In a moment I'm at Nate's table with a Spanish couple whom he introduces as Ozzie and Lourdes, his dear friends.

"And this is Serena," Nate says, "Very fortuitously, Serena and I happened to meet this afternoon at the winery."

"Oh, that's an excellent place for an accidental first meeting," Lourdes says. She has only a slight Spanish accent. "Ozzie and I met at – what do you call it? – a sex store."

She looks at Ozzie with a wicked smile.

He shrugs. "Well, I had a girlfriend at the time and I was going to buy her a birthday present."

"But you forgot about her right away, didn't you?" Lourdes laughs.

"Yes, I did!"

Nate laughs too. I feel somewhat uncomfortable, like I've jumped into a conversation that I'm not at all prepared for. But I really can't get away now that I accepted Nate's invitation, just like I felt I had to go along with the yoga class earlier.

Nate turns to me with a serious look. "I won't ask you if you've brought any sex toys with you on the Camino, Serena, because of the sanctity of this enterprise. But I've found that asking a woman about her sex toys can be an excellent icebreaker." Then he laughs. "That's a good name for a sex toy. The icebreaker!"

They're drinking sangria. Nate pours me a glass. These people seem so different from the members of my Camino group.

Or maybe I'm wrong. Natalie would probably – no, definitely! – love this conversation. There really isn't anything wrong with it, if you're in the mood. But I am *not* in the mood. Suddenly I feel like it's been a really long day.

I'm beginning to notice a pattern here. Whether it's with Natalie or Charlotte or now with this new person, Nate, I seem to find myself in somewhat uncomfortable conversations with rather self-absorbed people, and it's happening a lot more than I'd like. Is there something about me that's making this happen? Or are there just a lot more of this kind of person than there used to be?

There's also another thing that's happening too often. I find myself alone in my room wondering why I let people take advantage of me in these conversations. Right now, I'm tempted to go upstairs and stew about it. But I'm not going to do that. This time I'm going to take them on in their own game.

They're still amusing themselves making up names for sex toys.

"Excuse me," I say. "I want to mention how liberated I feel by finding myself with people who are talking about personal matters – intimate matters – in a frank and even humorous way. For me, this feels like a real opportunity to share some thoughts of my own along those same lines. I know we've just met but could I impose on you for some feedback?"

Nate leans toward me and touches my arm. "Thank you so much for saying that. I really appreciate that you haven't felt offended by our bawdy discourse. And please do share with us whatever you wish to share. You'll see that we're very good listeners."

He glances across the table at Ozzie and Lourdes. "Am I right, folks?"

"Yes, yes, by all means," Ozzie assures me.

I take a deep breath. "Okay, here goes. When my father was alive, he wintered off the coast of South America, and he always covered my family's travel expenses so we could spend a week or two with him. He also arranged to house us nearby, so we could share most meals together. It was easy to go back and forth between his place and ours and the kids and I loved this arrangement!

"One year, Richard, my husband, brought his new laptop with him. He had been working in my dad's office earlier in the day and that's where he left it when he went to play eighteen holes of golf.

While Richard was golfing, my dad and I were enjoying our time together on the patio. The kids asked him if they could play some games on the computer and my father told them, "Of course, go ahead, it's in my office." I think my father thought they were going to use his desktop computer, as did I!

"A few minutes later we heard a huge commotion from the office – it sounded like a combination of alarm, laughter and amazement all at the same time. They were saying, 'Mom, mom, come in here right now!'

I rushed in, expecting to see one of them had been hurt in some way. Instead, as I ran into the room, the kids were sitting in front of Richard's laptop, mesmerized by all kinds of really disturbing and extremely explicit porn on the screen!

I paused in my story then, as I could see that Lourdes wanted to ask a question.

"Excuse me," she said, "were there any videos of animals having sexual intercourse? Lions, for example?"

What a strange question. "No, I don't think there were any lions, Lourdes."

"Well, the reason I ask is, I once took our kids to the zoo – we have two kids, Simon and Simonetta – and the lions were having sexual intercourse. It had attracted quite a crowd and the kids were fascinated, so I explained to them what the lions were doing. Well, that night I looked on You-Tube for lions having sexual intercourse and I learned some amazing stuff. When the female lion goes into heat, the male lion has to fuck her every twenty minutes for a week! And if he won't do it, or can't do it, there is always another lion waiting in the wings!"

This anecdote from Lourdes led to a few minutes of joking around by Nate and his friends while I just sat there.

Finally Nate said, "Oh, excuse us, Serena. We're just being silly. Please continue with what you were saying."

"Yes, please excuse us," Ozzie begged.

So I went on. "There were a couple of amazing things about what was on Richard's computer. He was rarely interested in me sexually, so it was *shocking* that he had this very active fantasy life. Maybe it shouldn't have been a surprise, but it was. Also, at least half of the porn was homosexual."

Ozzie is fascinated. "But your husband was not *gay?*"

Before I can respond, Nate says, "Not to her knowledge, perhaps. But absence of evidence is not evidence of absence."

After this, I'd had enough. Between Natalie's bruised ego and this dinner conversation, I was ready to go to bed. Everyone in the dining room appeared to have been "over-served" and I was exhausted.

I politely excused myself, thanking them for including me, and headed up to my room. The rooms were small, but charming, and quite chilly. The temperature had been perfect during the afternoon, but by the time I got into bed it must have dropped thirty degrees! I closed the french doors to the balcony and found a blanket.

That night I sleep soundly, as I do most nights on the Camino. The next morning I am up by five a.m., then downstairs with my bags ready to be loaded into the van by six-thirty. I tell myself that today is a new day on the Camino, and a new opportunity to release the events of the past.

Chapter Twenty-Six

—◦◦◊◊◦◦—

When I signed up for the Camino I certainly wasn't expecting this kind of interpersonal complexity. Natalie has proven to be a really heavy load, and a full day with her, not to mention the time I'd spent with Nate and his friends was a lot for me to deal with.

I don't really feel *bad* about what went on with Nate, but I don't exactly feel good about it either. I have an inner sense that he is not who he is pretending to be. I can't put my finger on it, but my intuition tells me to be careful. I just don't trust him.

Now, nearly twenty-four hours after that dinner, I sit down to report on another day that has been very challenging, though in a different way.

It began around three o'clock this afternoon, as I was walking alone through an area of vineyards. Natalie and Charlotte had gone some distance ahead. Off to the left I noticed several structures that look like enormous beehives. They were architecturally beautiful, so I decided to step off the path and investigate further.

I moved as close as I could, climbed up a few feet and even managed to get some good shots on my phone. It's not until I was headed back toward the road that my trouble started.

Instead of heading to the spot where I had climbed up, I decided to jump down, a little further down the path. It was only a few feet high, but I lost my balance at the very moment I jumped. I fell forward as I landed, with my forearms taking the impact. Thank God I did not land on my hands, or both wrists would probably have been broken. I do remember sliding across the trail before passing out.

When I opened my eyes, I was face-down in the dirt. I didn't move at first; I just lay there trying to figure out what had just happened. Then I turned my head to the right, hoping to see another pilgrim coming from behind me, but nobody was in sight. I slowly began to move, and that's when I noticed all the blood. I was wearing a long- sleeved white top with a sleeveless one under it, and it was covered with blood mixed with the orange-colored earth common along the Camino.

I slowly stood up and peeled off the bloody long-sleeved top to reveal a series of cuts and scrapes, along with "road burn" on my right arm from my hand to my shoulder. One cut looked especially severe and was bleeding profusely.

Oddly enough, I didn't feel a lot of pain. I began to walk as fast as I was able. It took me about thirty minutes to catch up with Charlotte and Natalie.

They were deep in conversation and didn't even notice me until I asked if either of them had a moist cloth.

"Oh my God, what happened?" Charlotte asked, immediately opening her backpack. She then insisted on examining my nasty wound. First she poured water on a tissue, which she used to clean off the dirt, then followed up with an entire bottle of iodine. Lastly she wrapped the wound with some gauze she had in her pack.

I was so grateful for Charlotte's help that I really didn't know what to say, other than a promise to replace her gauze and bottle of iodine. Meanwhile, there was no cell phone service at that location so the three of us had to walk about another three miles to the outskirts of Santo Domingo.

As soon as we arrived in town, we stopped at the first café and order some iced tea, then Charlotte called Stella. Fifteen minutes later, Brutis pulled up in front and Stella jumped out. When I explained to her what happened, she told Natalie and Charlotte to head to the hotel, then she and I got into the van and went in search of a pharmacy.

It didn't take long to locate one, and as soon as the pharmacist looked at the wound he gave Stella directions to a nearby hospital and suggested that we go there at once.

Unlike back home, there was no waiting at the emergency room. Stella had already called Adam, who met us at the ER. Thank God I have guides who are fluent in Spanish!

As the doctor cleaned the puncture wound, he found a piece of quartzite that had embedded itself into the underside of my right elbow. It was fairly big, and I'm surprised it didn't go through my arm and come out the other side! After wrapping pretty much my whole arm in bandages, he gave me a tetanus shot and told us that I'll need to come back tomorrow.

After leaving the hospital, I realized that my watch was gone. I don't recall it coming off, but it must have gone flying when I had such a hard landing. It is the only valuable piece of jewelry I brought with me to the Camino, and when I mentioned it to Adam he immediately insisted that we try to find it.

We spent thirty minutes at the site of my fall but never found the watch. But that's not the end of it. Because it's an expensive watch, Adam pointed out that we needed to make a report at the police station so I can file an insurance claim.

Since Adam has a really good guidebook for all the towns along the Camino, finding the police station didn't take much time. It was a one-story brick building with a small parking lot that didn't have many cars. The place looked calm on the outside, but when we went in things were a lot different.

Chapter Twenty-Seven

—◦◦◇◦◦—

The whole atmosphere of the place was more like a railroad station than a police station. When we entered, lots of people were milling around in a single large room. A surprising number of them were young children, not all of whom were with an adult. Across the room the crowd thickened as people tried to talk to three uniformed guys behind a long counter.

Seeing this, I suddenly flashed a couple of insights about Spain. First, lots of people wear uniforms, especially the men, and it's not at all clear what the uniforms represent. Besides police officers, there are street sweepers, bus drivers, mail carriers, plus men of indeterminate occupations in unidentifiable uniforms. And, for some reason or another, they were all here in the police station.

Second, people in Spain and in many other countries don't connect with the concept of waiting in line. Instead, it's every man for himself in crowded environments. If this were a crowded police station in the United States, you'd have people automatically forming lines in front of the three policemen behind the counter. But that's not how it was here. There was just a general milling around in front of the counters, and the only way to get any help was to physically push your way through the crowd. It was like a football game, with the possibility at any moment that it could turn into a boxing match.

What were all these people doing here? Is there that much crime in such a small town? One thing was certain: I'm the only one who wanted to get a police report so I could file an insurance claim for my expensive watch.

Once Adam managed to speak to one of the guys behind the counter, there was a brief conversation in Spanish and things happened surprisingly fast. A policeman appeared beside us and led us toward a door at the far end of the room. As we pushed through the crowd I noticed that his uniform was a bit more elaborate than the guys behind the counter. He must have been a sergeant or something.

When we reached his tiny office, which resembled a small white box, the officer introduced himself as Sergeant Machado. That was the only English we would hear from him for the next three hours. Yes, it took three hours of back and forth Spanish conversation between Sergeant Machado, Stella, and Adam before I was able to walk out of the police station with the report in my hand. Incredible!

A big part of the problem was Sergeant Machado's ancient computer and, later, his ancient printer. As the three of us waited on folding chairs – my arm throbbing in pain – Machado continually switched from one screen to the next. Sometimes he turned the computer off and started over again. Occasionally the screen froze or went off altogether.

At one point Stella asked if Machado could simply write out a brief report in longhand, but Machado said that was impossible. The report had to be entered into the computer.

Finally he got it done. But he still had to print out the report so we could take it with us. With Adam as my translator,

I inquired if he could simply email the report to me. At first Machado looked puzzled, and then he looked sad. Unfortunately, that was impossible, he said, then, without further explanation he turned his attention to the printer.

It was ten p.m. when we finally arrived back at the hotel. I was shivering, my fever was climbing and the pain all over my body was getting worse and worse.

Chapter Twenty-Eight

—◦◦◇◦◦—

"I stood in the fire so long I became the flame."

~Author Unknown

The following day I do not walk, as I have to return to the hospital. When I get there the doctor explains that the wound can't be effectively stitched up due to the nature of the puncture. So he cleans it again and then informs me that the wound is infected. No big surprise there, as about four hours had elapsed between the fall and my arrival at the ER, where the wound was properly cleaned. The doctor prescribes some antibiotics and sends me off again.

I'd never thought about getting hurt while walking the Camino, and I certainly never imagined I would get such a serious injury. I feel embarrassed about it, and sorry to have been such a problem to the guides. The past two days have been completely taken up with my problems – from that first trip to the hospital and the search for my watch, to the marathon police report, the return to the hospital and finally, the long wait in line at the pharmacy. I hate being a nuisance, and I vow to make certain both Adam and Stella know how grateful I am for their help.

I also know that I won't be doing what several of the pilgrims in front of me at the pharmacy are planning. They are going home! One guy tripped on the roots that are everywhere on the Camino and broke four ribs! A young woman was stung by several bees and had an adverse reaction. Both tell me they have had enough and can't wait to get out of there! I know I will not let this stop me, or even slow me down. I have dedicated this time to completing this pilgrimage, and now, more than ever, I am determined to walk into Santiago.

Around nine p.m. Natalie comes to my room and announces she has an idea: we should sleep in tomorrow and take a cab to the next hotel. She suggests that we get settled and then walk backward along the route to the outskirts of Burgos, or even further if we feel like it.

I agree to this, partly because I know I'm going to have a hard time sleeping tonight. My arm really hurts, so I look forward to staying in bed past five a.m.

When I wake up around seven-thirty, I immediately check my phone for a message from Natalie. We had not decided on an exact time to meet, so I'm not surprised to see a message that was sent around seven. What does surprise me, although it probably shouldn't, is that Natalie has changed her mind. She's decided to just go ahead and walk the route.

I sigh, disappointed and more than a little annoyed. It's now too late for me to even think of leaving with the guides, who have already left the hotel. The more I think of what Natalie did, the angrier I am… at myself. I had let myself be manipulated by a specific kind of toxic personality, one that is very well described in a book called *The Wizard of Oz and Other Narcissists*:

The power of the narcissistic personality disorder person to bring you into unconscious agreement with her belief that she is someone truly extraordinary is possibly the most remarkable feature of the narcissist. Before you know what's happening, you may be following her lead, enjoying the charisma, or perhaps intimidated by her persuasiveness, power, and authority. You may not realize that you are losing track of your agenda and, at the same time, deferring to hers.

I had allowed Natalie to talk me into making this change of plans, and then when she didn't follow through on our agreement, I start beating myself up. I need to completely re-focus! I need to go back and reconnect with my original intention for walking the Camino by myself. I need to find the space and time and clarity I am hoping for.

By the time I get Natalie's text, it's too late for me to have breakfast, nor is there anybody around to help me bandage my arm. I pack up and call Adam, who says he'll pick me up at the hotel around ten. He also assures me that he will handle getting the bags into the van.

I'm still feeling angry as I struggle to get my bags down to the lobby. To make things as easy as possible for Adam, or perhaps to punish myself, I get my bags down the steep incline to the entrance of the hotel driveway where he'll pick me up. Because of my arm, this takes two trips.

By the way, it's a cold and rainy morning. There is no place to get out of the rain at the foot of the driveway. I have no gloves – I lent them to Natalie yesterday – and my hat is at the bottom of my bag. So is my rain jacket. And where the hell is Adam? This is incredible.

Now I have a choice to make. I can try to haul my bags back up the steep incline to the hotel lobby, or I can sit beside the driveway in a small enclosure that has a bench inside.

I decide on the small enclosure. Getting up the driveway with the bags would be impossible, and getting them into the enclosure is hard enough. At least there's a roof.

Sitting in here watching the rain, I feel like I'm really hitting bottom. I'm wet, I'm cold, my arm is hurting me and I have no idea when the van is going to show up. Or even if it *will* show up, because anything seems possible at this point.

Suddenly a very distinct memory comes to me, with every detail perfectly clear. But why does this happen? Is it just because I don't have anything else to do at the moment? Or is there some deeper reason?

This event occurred shortly after my divorce, when I was working in Chloe's boutique. I really enjoyed it, so much so that I was there six days a week. Like most stores, we stayed open late during the Christmas season so we could catch the after-work holiday shoppers. One night, a man walked in just as I was about to close up. He was an older man, probably in his mid-seventies, and said he was looking for a Christmas gift for his wife.

As I started to show him some things, he said, "You look familiar." He then tried to figure out places he might have seen me. When he mentioned being a member of the country club, I told him he may have recognized me from there. He then asked my name and I gave it to him – my married name – and he immediately connected me to Richard.

"Oh, I know all about you," he said.

I didn't quite like the way he said that. "What does that mean?"

As he started to answer, and once the momentary shock wore off, I had a realization. Richard had been telling everyone at the country club that I had done all the things that had actually been done by Richard himself. Richard was claiming that I was a drinker and that I was promiscuous – ALL of his behavior, not mine. Although I knew he was capable of terrible things, it was startling.

Before the man could say anything else, I said, "I need to stop you because what you've heard about me isn't me at all. I know you heard it from my ex-husband, and it's really all about him, not me. It doesn't matter to me whether you believe me or not, but everything you've just said is a projection. That's why I divorced my ex-husband. He was exactly the person you just described!"

This gentleman seemed to understand this truth. He said, "I believe you – but it's really sad, because the entire club thinks you are a terrible person."

I was certain it wasn't just the country club. I knew Richard was telling lies about me to as many people as he could. Since the divorce, I'd even had old friends say straight out, "We won't have anything to do with you." Now I knew why that had happened. Why hadn't I seen it before?

Adam doesn't arrive until one o'clock, after I had been sitting there for hours. He's very apologetic, saying he was delayed at a checkpoint. When he finally gets my bags into the back of the van and opens the door for me to climb in, I see, sitting in the front passenger side, none other than Natalie!

She is all smiles, rosy-cheeked from the warmth of the van. What is she so happy about? I sense that it's the feeling of power she has attained by driving me nuts. No, this is not what I had looked forward to on the Camino.

I get into the van and say nothing. Adam drops me at the agreed-upon checkpoint and I walk from there into San Juan de Ortega. From there, where we will be shuttled into Burgos, where we are staying at a lovely hotel for two nights.

I do love when we stay two nights in the same hotel. I send my laundry to the hotel cleaners, including my running shoes, which have turned the dark orange color of the soil. Sometimes I really can't stand putting my clean feet into those dirty shoes one more day! As for the white shirts I wore the day I fell, they're history. I threw them out after trying several times to wash the blood out.

Chapter Twenty-Nine

————◦◦◇◇◦————

After getting settled in my hotel room in Burgos, I take a hot bath and feel better. The rain has stopped and it's now a lovely evening, so I decide to walk into the city center. One of the many holdovers from Franco's long reign is that the time all over Spain is uniform and not geographically correct. During May in Burgos, the sun doesn't set until almost ten p.m. That's great for me because I rarely end a day of walking before six.

Perhaps because of some magnetic toxic vibration, Natalie is in the room next to me. She opens her door in her bathrobe just as I'm starting out.

She asks me what my plan is and I tell her that I plan to walk into the city and find a drug store so I can buy more bandages for my arm.

"Oh, let me give you a list of a few things I need!" she says, then hurries back into her room. When she returns a moment later with her list, I take it and head for the elevator as fast as I can.

Our hotel is downtown so there are lots of shops. So far the climate on the Camino has been mostly dry and windy and I need a moisturizer for my dry and peeling face.

I get what I need at a drug store, as well as Natalie's items. Surprise! Her list totals more than three hundred US dollars.

I get back to the hotel around nine o'clock, and then there's another surprise. As I'm opening the door to the lobby, I suddenly realize that someone is pushing it open for me from behind. I look over my shoulder, and see that it's Nate. For some reason I seem to encounter him a lot.

"Please, allow me," he says, referring to the door. He's smiling broadly. "You don't realize it, of course, but I've been madly looking for you, and now we're staying at the same hotel again. You've been right under my nose!"

I have no idea what to make of this. But since he's smiling I try to smile too. As we enter the lobby I say, "You've been looking for me?"

"I certainly have, and now we can spend a minute or two together without trying to include Ozzie and Lourdes in the conversation."

"Okay," I say, tentatively. "But why have you been looking for me?"

"Well, let's have a glass of wine and I'll explain. Don't worry, you're going to be very pleasantly surprised."

Nate seems positively buoyant, and I'm actually glad to have something that gets my mind off my damned arm. We sit on a sofa in a corner of the lobby, and a waiter instantly appears. Nate orders two glasses of red wine. He even tries to do it in Spanish, which is kind of funny.

"Gracias, señor," he says as the waiter takes the order, then he turns to me.

"Yes, I've been hoping to run into you, Serena."

So he's even remembered my name.

"Well, what's the surprise then, Nate?" I've remembered his name too.

Somehow managing to smile even more broadly, Nate reaches into the pocket of his jacket and produces my watch, the one I'd lost on the road when I hurt my arm.

My jaw drops. "Oh my God!"

"I'll bet you never thought you'd see this again."

In that moment I feel I could kiss him. I don't, of course, but I do give him a quick hug.

"May I?" he says, and he grasps my hand to put on the watch.

Wow. I'm so glad to have my watch back that my arm doesn't even hurt anymore. It's a real miracle cure.

Nate seems to be enjoying the moment as well. "So other than the watch, how have things been going?" he asks, then offers another "Gracias, señor" to the waiter, who has returned with the wine. We clink glasses and take a sip.

"You've been making good progress on the road?" he continues, "Not too strenuous, I hope."

"Oh, it's been fine," I say. But that doesn't seem enthusiastic enough. "I mean, it's been great."

Nate leans a few inches toward me. "Have there been any surprises?"

"Hm. Well, aside from meeting some new people, almost breaking my arm, losing my watch, and having my watch returned by a fine gentleman, I'd say it's been pretty much what I expected."

Nate sips his wine and nods thoughtfully.

"We come on a trip like this hoping for change, and expecting change. We're looking for a transformative experience, and that can happen. But at that same time, we learn that we can't change as fast as we want, not even on the Camino." He smiles gently. "Does that make any sense?"

"Actually, it does. It makes a lot of sense," I say, with a bit of a sigh. "Do you remember the story I told the other night, about my husband's… computer?"

"Yes, of course."

"One of the changes I hoped for on this trip was to free myself from the memories of my marriage. But I'm still being reminded of them. These memories are no longer serving any purpose and I am done with them!"

"I think I understand what you mean. I've felt that way myself sometimes. I even did some research on memory in general and memory of trauma in particular. Some really interesting stuff."

He takes another sip of wine, and since I haven't really touched mine I take a sip also. "Really? What did you find?"

It seems like a lot of what we call forgetting is really replacing. If we don't replace a memory with something else, that memory can remain vivid forever. And the more unique the memory is, the more difficult it is to replace. So we never forget how to ride a bicycle, because riding a bicycle is a unique experience, both physically and mentally. That's why it's easier to remember an unusual name than a really common one."

"Well, the so-called marriage between my ex and I WAS unique. That's for sure."

Suddenly, just when I was starting to get interested, Nate glances at his watch and gets to his feet. "Wow, it's later than I thought, Serena. I think we both need to get some rest." He takes some Spanish money out of his pocket and puts it on the coffee table in front of the sofa. "That ought to cover it."

I'm surprised by this abrupt conclusion, but then Nate comes up with a suggestion.

"Hey, I've got an idea," he says cheerfully. "I'm not much of a night person, but I'm an excellent morning person. What about you?"

"Yes, I'm definitely a pretty good morning person."

"Great. What about if we meet early tomorrow morning and take a walk by the Puente de San Pablo, an old bridge at the entrance to town that has some amazing sculptures. The Puente Santa Maria is also supposed to be wonderful. Those are places I've really wanted to see in Burgos, and if we get there early we can beat the crowd."

"Sure, that sounds good."

"Puente means bridge," he adds.

"I know."

Nate looks really pleased. I stand up and we share a quick hug. "Is seven too early for you?"

"No, that's fine. Then we can get back in time to start walking."

"Perfect! Let's meet in the lobby at seven." And he's gone. For some reason I really feel like drinking the wine now, so I sit back down and take a long sip.

About twenty minutes later I step off the elevator and head toward my room. Somehow, Natalie hears me coming down the hall, opens her door, and urgently inquires if I have the items from her list.

"Yes, I do." I've put her things in a separate bag along with the receipt. She thanks me, but (so far) the whole thing has cost her nothing.

Back in my room, I put some moisturizer on my face and then call down for room service. I haven't eaten all day and I'm starved, so I'm overjoyed when there's a knock on my door with a glass of wine and my salad. Great, great. I'm about to get into bed with my book when there's another knock on the door, and it's not a salad this time. It's, "Guess who?"

As soon as I open the door, Natalie asks me what I have on my face, then marches right past me towards my bathroom.

"Serena, I want to try your moisturizer," she says, and before I can say a word she has slathered way too much all over her face and neck.

This is very mysterious. Did she somehow know that I had bought the moisturizer? Is that possible? She's already on her way out. "And that's how we share!" she says, with what looks to me like an evil grin. Then she leaves.

I feel like I'm seeing Natalie's core personality emerge, a little more each day. I'm getting the picture of our relationship as a one-way street – her way – and I'm recognizing her keen ability to manipulate other people, which right now means myself and Charlotte. Even if I had seen this sooner, I'm not sure what, if anything, I could have done differently. Although we are four "solo" walkers, we actually are a collective group. There's the breakfast meeting each morning, and the common lodging each night, which requires a certain amount of involvement with each other. This is now day number twelve, and with twenty-three days to go I'm discovering "the truth" about Natalie. Is that a good thing? Maybe ignorance was bliss.

Chapter Thirty

Even before Nate suggested doing some sightseeing in Burgos this morning, I had decided to take the day off from the Camino. My arm continues to give me trouble and is making sleep difficult. Plus, this is by far the nicest hotel in which we've stayed, and I've been lucky enough to get an especially luxurious room. This will be a day to pamper myself a bit, and enjoy the beautiful and historic city. I'd have been happy to do it alone, but I'm also looking forward to seeing how things go with Nate.

We're both on time for our seven o'clock meeting in the lobby. "Do you want to grab a coffee before we leave," he asks, "or should we just get going?" I can tell he wants to head out right away, so I suggest we get something to eat near the historic bridge.

"What did you say the bridge is called?" I ask.

"Well, don't forget, there are actually two of them – Puente de Santa Maria and Puente de San Pablo. Both are very historic. We're really very close to Santa Maria now, so I thought we could take a cab to San Pablo and then walk back. We can also see the cathedral."

There are always cabs waiting in the hotel driveway, and there's always a doorman waiting for a tip. Nate has wisely anticipated this and has a tip ready as the doorman hails a cab with a grand gesture. A yellow Fiat arrives, and we're on our way.

It's a beautiful sunny morning. There's actually more traffic than I would have thought but the ride is still very pleasant. I'd thought Nate might try to converse with the driver in Spanish but after looking out the window for a moment he turns toward me and says, "Do I seem like a confident person? I mean, from your point of view as a woman, do I seem sure of myself?"

What a surprising question. But I can see that he's seriously awaiting my reply.

"Sure, I guess so. I mean, you seem appropriately confident." I feel like laughing. "Neither too much nor too little."

"That's good, thank you," Nate says, and he looks relieved. "I think there's an expectation that I'll be confident because of my Harvard degrees, and I also think women appreciate a confident, let's-get-the-show on the road kind of man. Is that true of you, Serena?"

"Well, I don't really know…"

"I'm afraid I may have seemed abrupt last night – the way I suddenly stood up to leave – but it's just that I felt the need to compose myself before we spoke anymore. I felt that way for myself – and also for you – because I'm very excited to have met you, and I don't want to disappoint you."

Wow, where is all this coming from? I'm not sure how to respond. Finally I say, "Do you feel composed now? You seem composed."

"Yes, I do feel that way. Thanks again," he concludes with another big smile, and in a few moments we're dropped off at the Puente de San Pablo.

It's really a beautiful site, and not one you'd expect to find in a modern city. The bridge, which is very wide, is surrounded by upscale apartments and office buildings; below it, the Rio Arlanzon flows through a lovely park. When you're on the bridge and looking down at the water you could just as easily be somewhere out in the countryside.

Both sides of the bridge are adorned with larger-than- life-size statues of medieval heroes, including the warrior El Cid, who was born in a town a few miles from Burgos and at various times fought for both Christians and Muslims. The bridge used to be the entrance to the city, and it's on the route of the Camino. Looking at these magnificent statues I find myself appreciating the events, as unpleasant as some had been, that led me to spending time here.

We walk across the bridge and then turn left through another beautiful park. It's not a very long walk back toward the Puente Santa Maria, and both of us are content to just enjoy the setting. I'm just as glad not to be talking, because I've gotten to know Nate well enough to expect plenty of talking soon enough.

Puente de Santa Maria is much narrower than the other bridge, and it's closed off to cars. Maybe that's why it looks so genuinely medieval. Our hotel is to the south of the bridge, and now we're at the north end where there's a huge and very ornate ceremonial archway that was once a gate to the old city. It was originally built in the Middle Ages and then reconstructed by Charles V, the powerful emperor who in the sixteenth century ruled both Spain and the Netherlands. There are a number of large statues on the archway, which for some reason doesn't surprise me, and several have swords in their hands. They're all men, which doesn't surprise me either.

Beyond the archway is the cathedral, the third largest in Spain. From the outside it's an imposing structure, and I'm sure the inside is spectacular. But before we undertake that we decide to have our light breakfast in one of the many cafés near the river.

Nate orders an omelet and I'm having a croissant and a cup of coffee. One interesting thing about Nate is that he's often very talkative but he's also an excellent listener. There's something paradoxical about that and I haven't seen it in many other people. Or maybe he was just that way with me. Anyway, when I start telling him about my encounter with Natalie in my room the night before, I can tell he's listening very closely. He even nods his head a couple of times.

"I'm starting to feel that I need to protect myself from her, but there are also times when I really do enjoy her company.

I've been thinking about this a lot because of what happened in my marriage, which is very typical of being in a relationship with a person with a narcissistic personality disorder. Natalie seems like that type of person."

Since Nate seems to be giving me his full attention, I continue on a bit. "What happens when I'm involved with a narcissistic personality? I feel frustration, confusion, fear, exhaustion, uncertainty, inadequacy, neglect, disempowerment, and loneliness. I'm sure there's more but you get the idea. Whew!"

I take a deep breath and manage to end this with a smile, but Nate looks very serious.

"So you have a psychological perspective on your experience with these people. Do you find that helpful? I mean, does it seem more helpful than if you thought that a sorcerer had put a spell on them?"

"What?" Is this a joke? I have to laugh, but Nate still has a serious expression. "For some reason the possibility of a sorcerer never occurred to me, Nate."

"I mention that because in college I had a class with a famous anthropologist. He'd spent years living with indigenous groups in the Amazon. If somebody in the group started acting in an antisocial way, they would assume it was caused by a sorcerer's spell, so they'd have an exorcism ceremony. If that didn't work, they'd sneak up behind the guy and kill him."

"Very good. Are you trying to give me ideas?"

"Well, I guess I'm trying to say that there are different ways of looking at these kinds of people, and different terminologies we can use. Narcissist is the one we use now, and in the past we might have called them a zombie or something. The main thing is we want to feel we have some understanding and control of the situation."

"Okay. But aside from hitting Natalie over the head with a stone axe, is there anything I can do?"

He shakes his head. "I really don't think so. There's no point in trying to change a person like that. I know you want to complete the Camino, so maybe just try to keep your distance as much as possible."

"Well, as much as possible isn't much."

"Alas!"

"Yes, alas."

The rest of our conversation is in a lighter vein. The cathedral is looming beyond the archway, so we don't linger in the café because masses of tourists are sure to show up soon. When we arrived at the cathedral, it turns out our timing was perfect because the day's first tour is just beginning.

As our uniformed guide explains, a Romanesque church on this site was built in the eleventh century, but it was torn down in the thirteenth century because Burgos was booming and deserved a full-fledged Gothic cathedral. Over the course of the next five hundred years, even into the nineteenth century, the present-day cathedral of Burgos was worked on and then worked on some more.

During earlier trips to Europe, I'd visited the most celebrated cathedrals of France. I would never say that if you've seen one cathedral you've seen them all, but seeing cathedrals is a kind of cumulative experience so that when you see a new one it's never completely new, but a continuation of the ones you've seen before. The bottom line is you – or at least I – can start to feel satisfied pretty quickly, which is not to take anything away from the grandeur of the cathedral itself. This is what I realize during our tour.

Our guide, who is a consummate professional after doing this God knows how many times, speaks first in rapid- fire Spanish then repeats himself more slowly in English, with a moderately heavy accent. This takes four hours.

After that, Nate and I are pretty much out of gas. Nate tips the guide, who also looks exhausted, though this may be a way of signaling that he'd made a mighty effort. Then we step back out into the sunlight.

Chapter Thirty-One

—◦◦◇◇◦◦—

We don't talk much on the way back to the hotel. In the past few hours there has been lots of talking, and even though it was the guide who was doing it, Nate and I are ready for a few minutes of silence. It's still a beautiful afternoon, and the walk back across the Santa Maria bridge is a great way to enjoy it.

As we approach the hotel, I tell Nate that this has been a really enjoyable day. I mean it, too. Taking this time off from walking was a good idea, and I'm glad I had someone to share it with.

Nate seems extremely happy to hear this. In fact, he actually looks thrilled. He stops walking and turns toward me, and I'm suddenly enveloped in a hug.

After a moment he takes a step back, still smiling. Then, somehow, his smile changes slightly. "Serena," he says, "could you do something for me? Could you please hold up your right hand?"

"Sure," I say. "That seems simple enough."

"Great. Now I'm going to touch your hand with my hand." He hesitates for a moment, then continues, "And when I touch your hand, I want you to know that I'm doing this with an erotic intention, a Tantric consciousness. It's different from a goodbye hug. It's really a kind of hello."

Before I can say anything – not that I would have known what to say – Nate touches my hand. A long moment passes. He closes his eyes, then opens them again and now his old smile is back.

"Thank you," he says. "Thank you!"

As we continue on toward the hotel, Nate unexpectedly stops again. He takes an envelope from the pocket of his jacket.

"I'm afraid I have one more request. I hope you'll read this when you have a moment."

Without another word, he hurries off into the hotel, leaving me standing there with the envelope in my hand, and questions about this very odd fellow swirling in my mind.

I get back to my room in the hotel without encountering anyone from our group. Not that I expected to, because they're all out there Camino-ing. As for me, I set the envelope aside and decide to check my emails instead. Though I am curious, I have a sneaking suspicion I won't be pleased by what it contains. By the time I finish responding to the necessary emails and pay some bills, and it's nearly six o'clock.

Should I go downstairs for dinner? At first I'm not sure, but then Nate's envelope on top of the television makes the decision for me. It literally chases me out of the room, as if it were radioactive. I had thought about taking a quick shower, but no!

Chapter Thirty-Two

——◦◦◇◇◦◦——

I start the day walking with Natalie, and we get confused about the correct road out of Burgos. That's easy to do, especially in places on the Camino Frances that most pilgrims avoid because the signs are often just a faded yellow arrow on the dusty path.

Today a fork in the path is not marked at all, and we end up going off the correct route. It's the kind of day when the wetness goes right to the bone. We're soaked and shivering, walking as fast as we can to create some heat, when we spot a stone building up ahead. We don't know what it is, and at this point we don't care – we just want to go inside to warm up and dry off. The dampness has created a deep and painful throbbing in my arm, and though I have pushed through it all day I know it's time to stop.

The building turns out to be a small church, or more like a chapel, with room for about a dozen people at most. When we enter, there are lots of small candles twinkling and "Ave Maria" is softly playing. This is just what the doctor ordered!

A nun is standing by the door to welcome each pilgrim. She offers us a blessing and places a medal on a string around our necks. I feel something special here, a sense of true Grace and love. Once we've warmed our hands, we go to thank the nun, who gives each of us a blessing. It is such an uncredible, unexpected gift.

Now Natalie and I decide to part ways. This is a common occurrence among solo walkers, and nobody is offended when another desires to go it alone. Thirteen miles later, I meet up with our group and other pilgrims outside Bar Manolo, in the small town square of Hornillos, where Adam and Stella will eventually collect us. The day has gone from cold and wet to a beautiful, sunny and warm evening, so in the meantime we grab a table with a small cathedral behind us and order some drinks.

For the next hour we just relax, laugh, and share stories, and by the time Brutis pulls up I am feeling calm, peaceful, and more than ready to head for the ancient town of Castrojeriz.

I have not made many comparisons between Spain and the U.S., but I find this delightfully sleepy town, with its population of just five hundred, reminiscent of Jerome, an old mining town in Arizona. Castrojeriz has several ruined castles and monasteries, and some Roman and Visigothic ruins. It rose to prominence during the *Reconquista*, the long-standing war between Christians and Muslims, and is a major stopping place on the medieval Camino, with no less than eight pilgrim hostels.

We're staying in a gorgeous home that has recently been renovated by a doctor friend of Adam's. I'm not sure exactly when the original structure was built, but this is a medieval town, so I assume the structure dates from the seventh or eighth century.

Sandra, the owner, had clearly hired a very experienced and creative architect, because the entire five-story *posada* is spectacular. This evening, Sandra gives us a tour of the building. Under the building there's a system of interconnecting caves that likely date back to the first century. She had begun excavating the caves, but had to stop because the work became too costly. It was discovered, however, that the entire town was connected via these underground caves, which had collapsed on themselves over the centuries. Sandra has since created a wine cellar out of the cave beneath the building.

After some wine on an outside stone patio, we have dinner in the posada's spacious dining room with its windows overlooking the mountains. Charlotte doesn't join us for dinner tonight – I'm assuming she's too tired – and Natalie sits with the rest of us but just has some more wine. After the first course, she makes a big show of suddenly getting up and taking food upstairs to Charlotte, explaining she's her "nurse."

I watch her exit the room, once again struck by her lack of consideration. Sandra had specifically asked how many people would be eating dinner, and Natalie had led her to believe that she would one of them. Clearly she feels endlessly entitled to special consideration and attention. What's more, I believe Adam and Stella are also getting tired of her antics.

Chapter Thirty-Three

Another beautiful, sunny day. I walk alone much of the time. About 7.5 kilometers after leaving Castrojeriz, I come to a bridge – "Puente de Itero" – that crosses the Rio Pisuerga from the Burgos region into the Provincia de Palencia. The river provides the natural historical boundary between the old kingdoms of Castilla and Leon.

The Camino winds up and down and all around the extensive farmlands, with rivers and canals irrigating the rich soils. As I near Boadilla del Camino, a typical rural community along the Camino, I catch up with Kelly, the co-owner of the travel group who had joined us the night before to see how we are enjoying the Camino. Kelly lives north of the Camino and is responsible for most of the office work, allowing Vivienne to serve as a guide and run the bar/café she owns about twenty-five miles outside of Santiago. Kelly and I begin walking together after meeting at the parish Church of Santa Maria XVI.

I know from our previous conversations that Kelly and I have had similar experiences with toxic relationships. Like me, she too has children with an alcoholic, and now talk turns to the lengths we have gone through to protect our kids from their fathers' drinking. As I listen to her speak I am filled with sympathy. Her children are still small, and though her decision to leave the relationship was undoubtedly the right one, she now had her work cut out for her as a single mom.

After walking the remainder of the relatively "easy" day of sixteen miles into Fromista, Kelly and I go our separate ways.

As I walk into the lobby, I find Natalie and Charlotte already showered and dressed for dinner. It's an especially lovely evening, and I tell them I will meet them out as soon as I clean up and call home.

About an hour later, refreshed from a hot shower, I meet the girls in the town square. I don't feel like eating so the three of us stop at a couple of outdoor bars, visit a cathedral, take photos in front of a fountain, and laugh a lot. I let them know that I haven't had this much fun with other women since my college years.

It's around nine-thirty when we return to the hotel. Shortly after I get into my room there's a knock on my door. It's Natalie, standing there with the open pilgrim guide book in her hands. She reads out loud, "Today we have our first taste of the somewhat soulless *sendas* (pilgrim autopistas) that run alongside the main roads." Autopistas, I know, are like highways and very busy, therefore less than desirable for those seeking a serene experience on the Camino.

She then suggests that we do what we had planned the week before: take a cab to the next hotel, then walk backward along the route. I hesitate for a moment – my ordeal when she canceled last time still fresh in my mind – but then I hear myself agreeing. As soon as she leaves I start questioning my decision. I know I can't trust her, and that my only choice is to cover my bases. Before I slip into bed that night my bag is packed and ready to go.

Chapter Thirty-Four

———◦◦◇◦◦———

As you are shifting, you will begin to realize that you are not the same person you used to be..."

~Author Unknown

The next morning I drop my bags in the lobby and arrive at the breakfast meeting dressed to walk. As I listen to Adam tell us what to expect during the day, as he or Stella do every morning, I realize that Natalie isn't there. She makes her entrance just as the meeting ends – and what an entrance it is!

"You!" she screams at the top of lungs, her finger pointing at me. "You made me look like a fool! You humiliated me!"

Wow! And just how did I do that? She thinks it's because her bags were not with everyone else's in the lobby, and mine were.

Everything in the dining room comes to a halt. All eyes are on Natalie. She seems completely out of control, but the truth is, she is completely *in control*. Natalie has now had seventeen days to assess my role in her pursuit of power and this scene is her payoff for it.

Power is the goal of all narcissists. They see relationships as continuous power struggles, and they must always win those struggles. Natalie has apparently decided that I am a threat, a competitor. And on this particular morning, she has begun her all-out assault on me.

I knew I could not trust her. I saw her narcissistic tendencies. But I was NOT prepared for warfare!

Still, I walk toward her, place my hands on her shoulders and say, "Natalie, calm down!" What are you talking about?"

This further infuriates her. Her voice is even louder, her fury is more intense. "Look at you!" she screams, "You are dressed to walk today! Your bags are in the lobby! You have deliberately made me look like an idiot in front of all these people!"

With a sweeping gesture, she includes everyone in the dining room. I am speechless. I have no idea what the hell she's talking about.

"Natalie, I'm sorry if you feel this way. But I don't understand. Yes, my bags are in the lobby and I am dressed to walk today, because that is what we agreed to do last night! Remember? Walk backwards from the next village!"

This does nothing to placate her. She turns toward the onlooking crowd and says, "She did this to me on purpose! "

Well, I've had enough. As I walk out into the lobby she continues her monologue, and I can't believe my ears.

"Serena came into my room last night! She had the Camino map book! She told me today's walk would have no soul and that we should take a taxi to the next village!"

What?! I go back to my room, furious but for the first time absolutely clear about who I am dealing with.

Just five days earlier, when Natalie set me up and left me alone in the hotel, I was angry but I didn't really blame her.

Instead, I beat the shit out of myself for allowing her to trick me! But from *her* perspective, she had tested me and came to the conclusion that I was a perfect target.

What had tripped me up, I realize, is that I had been uncertain of her intent. Like any target of a narcissist, I had allowed Natalie's charm and charismatic display of humor, drama and wit to put me off balance. Now I know I need to refocus and be an adult. I need to take personal responsibility and not allow Natalie or anyone else to manipulate me ever again. I no longer will play this game!

When I return to the dining room, Natalie is complaining to Charlotte that I had "tricked" her. She's projecting her behavior onto me, just as Richard had done at our country club.

Then Natalie looks at me and decides to change her tactics. It's really kind of brilliant how she can come up with this stuff.

"Aw, come on, Serena, we're just having a girly fight!"

What I should have said is, "Natalie, I'm not a girl. I'm a grown woman!" But I'm never quick on my feet when caught off guard by these kinds of people, so I simply reply that I had not planned to leave her behind, and I had not broken my word to her about the previous night's plan. Then I tell her I'm going to get us a cab. The rest of the group is about to leave on foot.

While Natalie returns to her room to gather her things, Stella and Adam ask me if I'm okay. I assure them that I'm fine, that I'll see them that evening.

A few minutes later, Natalie and I are riding in silence toward the next lodging – it's an ancient monastery, enormous and beautiful. We arrive too early to access our rooms, so I ask the woman at the desk if I can leave my bags with her while we look around and she agrees.

I begin walking in the direction of the monastery's cloisters, with Natalie following some distance from me. I am disgusted with her, and I know that I will have to deal with her for the next three weeks. I feel anxious and alone. I also feel stupid about falling for her charming and convincing "courting" of me. I know I had to come up with a plan.

First, I need to tell her that her behavior is unacceptable. I will never again allow this to happen.

Second, until we reach Santiago, I intend to behave like an adult and not involve myself and others in her childlike antics.

Third, regardless of her behavior and how I've responded to it in the past, I'm onto her now. I will be polite and civil, but there will be no more plans, no more dinners, no more anything. I need my space and my time. She needs to respect this and stay away from me.

Once I'm able to get my bags into my room in the monastery, I spend the afternoon walking the Camino in reverse. That night, in the village square, I have a salad in an outdoor café, alone, but in peace. When I return to the monastery I get my bag packed and myself ready for bed, but I don't slip between the covers. First, I have an email to write. Before I know it, my fingers are flying over the keys of my computer.

Natalie,

I've now had repeated lessons about standing up for my truth and not accepting unkind, and/or cruel behavior from others.

Speaking from my experience, people treat me the way I *allow* them to treat me. I choose to be honest and clear with people, and also to communicate with kindness. On the outside

I may appear soft, and I actually am! I do my best to never hurt or harm anyone. You claim that you had a bad day today. OK. But I do not accept being used as your emotional garbage bin. I was in shock and utterly confused when you unleashed your loud and public and UNTRUE judgment about me. I apologized to you only because I hate emotional outbursts and I wanted to calm you down.

In hindsight, I had absolutely nothing to apologize for. The idea that I had somehow caused you to look like a fool was your belief and not a fact. Nobody makes anyone look like anything. We are all responsible for how we appear to others. I am not the type of person to ever do anything like what you accused me of doing.

That being said, it was a good reminder for me. I allowed you to rob me of more than an entire day on this Camino. To be clear, I am not blaming you for anything other than behaving badly. I take responsibility for giving away too much of myself to you, causing me a day filled with feelings of misunderstanding and confusion as well as betrayal. I need to re-focus and be clear with you that I will not accept that kind of treatment from you or anybody else, Camino or no Camino! I am worthy of being treated the way I treat you – with honesty and kindness.

I hope we can agree to move forward with this in mind. I also need to put more space around me each day while walking. I have learned that I am responsible for me in every way and when I am hurt I need to protect myself.

I would enjoy sharing some meals with you and Charlotte but should you not also want this, I accept your choices.

Serena

As soon as I send the message, I realize it was way too long and much too generous. Her eyes will probably glaze over by the third paragraph. What I really should have written is something more like this:

GO FUCK YOURSELF! I SEE YOU! Don't fuck with me ever again. If you try, you will discover that while you may believe yourself to be clever, I am actually extremely intelligent. And that discovery, Natalie, will cause you more regret than your self-centered, small mind can ever handle!

Chapter Thirty-Five

—◦◦◇◦◦—

*"When the power of love overcomes the love of power,
the world will know peace."*

~Jimi Hendrix

The following day I don't see Natalie until she and a few others get a table for lunch in a garden café along the Camino. Strangely, Natalie seems thrilled to see me.

"Serena!" she yells, the ever-present wine glass in her hand, "Come join the party!"

I have no idea how such a small woman can consume her daily volume of alcohol and keep moving. Actually, more often than not, after lunch she announces it's "too hot" or "I ate too much." Then she hops into the van and gets a ride to that night's hotel or inn. By the time we return after a day of walking, she's showered, changed, and has already finished a bottle of wine.

Today I decline Natalie's invitation to join the party. Instead, I quickly explain that I'm just about to leave. And that is exactly what I do.

When I arrive back at the monastery, I go directly to the bar for an iced tea. Charlotte and Natalie are there drinking wine.

Incredibly, or maybe not, Natalie starts in on me again. She's back to insisting that I made a fool of her the day before.

I look straight at her and say, "STOP!" and she gets up and walks away.

About fifteen minutes later she's back. Now, with tears in her eyes, she claims that she'd just read my email and is sincerely sorry for the events of the day before. She had been wrong, she said; she was taking out her hurt feelings on me after a difficult phone call from "home." Home was a code word that could refer to either her husband or her lover. Whoever it was from, the phone call had deeply upset her.

Finally, Natalie says she genuinely cares about me and hopes I can find it in my heart to forgive her.

I agree to do that, mostly because it seems like the most pragmatic response, considering the time we still have left on the Camino. Despite her apologies and declarations, I know her behavior is not going to fundamentally change. On the contrary, she'll probably become more manipulative and maddening with each passing day. With narcissists, it cannot be any other way.

Chapter Thirty-Six

———◇◇◇◇◇———

Today is a day to rejoice in the simple pleasures. I have clean laundry again! Clean running shoes, too, thanks to the hotel staff. When they're returned to me, they look brand new. The reddish brown of the Spanish earth is gone and the shoes are back to their original white.

We're in Leon, which was originally a Roman military garrison and base for its *Legio VII* (Seventh Legion), hence the name. It later became the capital of the old kingdoms of Asturias and Leon. Ancient and modern influences share the banks of the Rio Bernesga. The city, like the river, absorbs it all in an eclectic embrace.

After a day of exploration we are gifted with a beautiful, orange-colored full moon. Our hotel is an old apartment building that has been renovated and re-purposed. From my room on the top floor, I can see the gigantic orb, shining big and bright.

Earlier, Natalie had spotted a French restaurant and inquired whether they served dinner before nine p.m. According to Natalie, she was told seating would be available at eight-thirty. She texts me, asking if I want to join her. We are craving ANYTHING other than northern Spanish cuisine, so

I agree, even though I know we will never get back to the hotel before eleven.

Natalie comes to my room around eight and we walk through the old city. At the restaurant, we give the hostess Natalie's name and are asked to sit at the bar until our table is ready. At eight-thirty, we're the only people in the restaurant.

After a glass of wine, Natalie asks about the table and is told, "In one minute." I expect that will actually mean one hour, and in fact we're not seated until after nine. The menu looks superb, however. After we order, I ask Natalie to explain why her Camino is a "walk of gratitude," which is what she had told the group at dinner our first night. I'm curious, what does she feel especially grateful for?

By now she's had two or three glasses of wine, so she is more than willing to tell me all about it. Her Camino, she says, is a pilgrimage of gratitude because she is married to a wonderful man!

The wonderful man is a successful businessman. He owns his own company and is well-known in his field. Because of his position, Natalie is not comfortable telling me his name (she goes by her maiden name). She venerates his intelligence and tells me how much respect she has for his success. (I conclude she enjoys the prosperity his business provides her with!)

She then goes on to tell me that she and her husband have traveled all around the world. She talks to me about her travels as if I've never left my own backyard. (Why am I surprised by her superiority?)

But her husband is just one of her reasons for gratitude. The other is her lover!

When Natalie finishes the Camino and enters Santiago, her lover – "Mister X" – will be waiting for her in a hotel suite he has reserved for them, Natalie cannot say enough wonderful things about this guy either. I recall that earlier she'd told me he was quite a bit younger than she. She had also told me that he is a blood relative of her husband's! (Truth *is* stranger than fiction!)

Now she goes into some detail of the joys of having a younger lover, especially one who worships you. Mister X has declared that he will never marry, because nobody could ever compare to Natalie: her beauty, her brains, her elegance, her knowledge of the world. Yes, he is destined to remain her lover, since Natalie has made it clear she will never leave her husband.

As she spins this tale, I feel sorry for Mister X, who has written off ever having his own family. Someday he may regret this. But Natalie is proud of the whole thing. She's so puffed up about it that she almost seems to be rising out of her chair.

When I can't help mentioning my concerns about Mr. X, Natalie reminds me that everything is his own free will. So, tut tut, Serena.

Then I make a big mistake. Because I'm weary of Natalie's soap opera, I can't resist sharing some drama of my own. It's just to show her that she's not the only one, I guess.

"Just this morning," I tell her, "I received a text from a man named Michael. He was very close to me at one time. He's suffering from a broken heart."

This seems to perk her up.

"You broke his heart?" she asks hopefully.

"I hope not! I certainly never had any intention of breaking his heart, or anyone else's! We met while taking a semester abroad during college, which I had done mostly to escape my parents' divorce."

"So you went to Europe?" Natalie asks.

I nod. "Yes, my school offered it, as do many universities. It was actually my mother's suggestion. She felt I should get away for a while."

I pause for a moment as the memories begin to come back. This is about a point in my life that I haven't thought about for a long time.

"Michael and I were pretty much inseparable for three and a half months," I conclude.

"That's wonderful," Natalie says. "Did you have sex under the stars in a far-off land?"

I choose to ignore this and go on with the rest of the story.

"When we returned to the U.S. I was really sad. Why couldn't we stay away forever? I wasn't prepared to deal with my father's grief or my mother's expectation that I support her decision to leave. I was also stressed out about taking an especially challenging class required for my major. I would be attending a university near my childhood home for much of the summer.

I take a deep breath. "I knew what I had to do, and I would do it. But I couldn't continue a romance that had begun in another country. The two realities, for whatever reason, could not coexist for me. That was more than I could handle.

"Richard, with whom I had a prior relationship, planned to come visit me after I returned home. But for whatever reason, I was not ready to see him again.

Natalie nodded in appreciation. "That's a real drama. It's like *Casablanca*, except the farewell scene is different. Do you know that old film? Humphrey Bogart is the star?"

Once again I choose to ignore her flippant comment. It's difficult for her to listen to someone else's story, probably because she's counting the seconds until she can get back to her own. This is exactly why I keep going.

I tell her I simply was not ready to be back home, which no longer resembled the only one I'd ever known. I loved the peace of being thousands of miles away, far from the chaos created by my mother. I was literally sick every night as the end of my semester away approached.

"I was happy to see my dad again. I was living with him that summer. When I got back, he asked about my trip and I told him about some of the highlights. We did talk often about the divorce. My poor father was still trying to make sense of it all! He needed me to listen. I could empathize, as we both felt like we had been rejected and abandoned!"

"Did you inform him about Mickey?"

"Michael. No, I did not."

Another thoughtful nod. "I think you were very wise. It's difficult for a father to accept his daughter's sexual blossoming. I'm sure it's even worse when the father is being deserted by his wife, he's so alone."

"Um, yes. But I'd rather not go there..."

"Did you say she was departing with a new boyfriend? How humiliating. On the one hand he's got his daughter experimenting with sexual positions and so forth, and on the other hand he's got his wife rediscovering her orgasmic potential with a new flame. And meanwhile, as I said, he's alone. Did you find any *Playboy* magazines around the house?"

Oh my God. I can't take it anymore, but I do my best. I listen to Natalie's soap opera and then try to beat her at her own game. But she wins. She's just too horrible, too ruthless. After some mumbled explanation I get up and leave. Is she offended? I hope so. It's the most I can hope for.

—

Chapter Thirty-Seven

———◦◦◇◦◦———

I start out on Sunday walking with the group. It's another beautiful day, sunny and cool. The spring grass is bright green and all the plants are in blossom, a gorgeous display of color! As we walk out of Leon, we pass the Cathedral Pulchra Leonina, which takes up the entire east side of the Plaza Regal. It's a thirteenth-century Gothic cathedral renowned for its one hundred and twenty five magnificent stained glass windows.

Next, we come to the Plaza San Marcos, with an ancient monastery dedicated to St. Mark. The facade has many pilgrim motifs, including the sword of Santiago entwined with the lion of San Marcos. I get a great photo of a medieval pilgrim sitting at the base of the stone cross, resting his weary feet.

We pass over the Rio Bernesga to our first checkpoint, and from there we cross the Rio Oncina en route to our lunch stop in a small village called Chozas de Abajo.

I walk the remainder of the day alone through fields of red poppies and ancient, tiny hamlets, each with its own church and bell towers. Each tower along the Camino is inhabited by storks that build enormous nests for their newborn chicks.

The day of walking ends in Villar de Mazarife. The group meets up at a bar in the village center. We count four baby storks in just one of several nests at the top of the bell tower.

My last photo of the day is taken at a lovely outdoor café. It's around eight p.m. and the sun is still shining bright.

Chapter Thirty-Eight

I'm walking alone. My music for today is Chris Williamson's rendition of "Tender Lady" because I know I'll be quite a tender, sore, exhausted, dusty, hot and sweaty lady by the end of the day.

This is the longest day – thirty-one kilometers! – on the Camino. I'm going through fields, desert and farmland. I cross the Puente de Orbigo, one of the longest and best preserved medieval bridges in Spain. It dates back to the thirteenth century, when it was constructed over an earlier Roman bridge. It's one of the great historical landmarks on the Camino.

After a checkpoint at "Hospital De Orbigo," I reach our planned lunch spot in a beautiful outdoor garden at Santibanez de Valdeiglesias. I sit with Charles and Adam, watching the birds. It's another sunny day, and a hot one!

Today's second checkpoint is La Casa de los Dioses Cantina, one of the more serene and naturally beautiful pathways of the Camino. So much to admire, but by midafternoon I'm starting to feel tired. After crossing the Rio Tuerto and walking along some paths of red clay, I finally reached our hotel in Astorga. By this time I'm exhausted and thirsty and starved. At the hotel I'm surprised (but not really) to learn that Natalie had not walked another step after lunch.

I quickly wash up and eat dinner at a café in the town square. I'm proud that I walked the entire route today. But I promise myself to never hike that many miles again!

Chapter Thirty-Nine

———◦◦◇◦◦———

I wake with my injured elbow extremely red, swollen and hot to the touch. This, despite having finished a full, ten-day course of antibiotics and diligently cleaning and rebandaging the wound each day. I had thought it was making progress, however slowly, but now I'm wondering.

When I arrive at our breakfast meeting Stella takes one look at the elbow and comments on its size and color. I need to see a doctor, she says, immediately.

Adam, who has just entered the dining room, comes over to see what was going on. He's surprised by how bad the elbow looked and, over my protestations, joins Stella in insisting I seek medical care. They wear me down, and after breakfast Adam and I climb into the van in search of an open clinic. It takes us some time, and directions from several locals, to find one in this funny little town.

We are both perplexed when we arrive at the address in a desolate corner of town. It is an odd building, and nothing like any medical facility Adam or I have ever seen.

It's raining lightly and cool, but my chill, I know, is due to a climbing fever from the infection. We walk around the building and finally find an open door. Adam does the talking as nobody in these remote villages speaks much English.

We are directed into an exam room, where two male doctors are waiting. They start talking, in Spanish too fast for me to understand, and after about ten minutes of back and forth Adam tells me they need to open the wound and drain it. I hop up on an exam table and take off my jacket, exposing my pitiful elbow. Then, with no advance warning, one of the doctors takes a scalpel and cuts open the wound, draining the infected fluid.

Adam looks at me with wide eyes, surprised at how fast this doctor works. I just turn my head away from what he's doing. It hurts, but what could I do? After he had drained the wound and cleaned it again, he wraps my arm in another bandage and sends me into an adjoining room where another doctor is waiting.

This doctor is writing out a prescription for another antibiotic. At the same time, Adam is telling me that my arm has a serious secondary infection and it was lucky we saw these doctors today.

The doctor I saw when I first got hurt spoke English. He had carefully explained everything to me, including the name of the antibiotic. I was familiar with this medication and took it as prescribed. This time, between the language barrier and pain, I don't think to ask Adam to translate what the medication is. I just want to get it into my body and get this whole thing over with.

We find a pharmacy and are both surprised when they charge me just three Euros for the ten-day supply. I immediately pop a pill and, again, apologize to Adam for this inconvenience. I also thank him for his help and his patience! We then set off for the first checkpoint where I will begin walking.

Around midday, I get a wonderful surprise – a Facetime call from my daughter with whom I haven't spoken in several days. As usual, I'm walking by myself and I keep using the phone to give her panoramic views of my surroundings, hoping she can get a sense of the beauty and peace of this land.

After talking for about forty-five minutes, she begins to sound concerned. She likes seeing the countryside, but she wonders why there are no other people. I explain that much of the Camino Frances is in a very rural area of northern Spain. The towns are small. The only "tourists" are the pilgrims walking the Camino.

She asks, "But why don't I see any of the others?"

I reply that few people actually walk the entire Camino, especially this time of year. Many pilgrims walk during the summer months, in particular Europeans who typically have a full month off in the summer . Also, many groups of pilgrims only walk the last hundred kilometers in order to get an official certificate of completion. The relative few who start off in France this time of year are doing so precisely because they prefer to walk alone most of the way.

She asks if I'm ever frightened, being by myself most of the time. But I'm never afraid. Compared to all the other well-known treks across the world, the Camino Frances is the safest one, and definitely safest for a solo female.

I don't tell her about my arm.

After the call ends, I start to feel tired. Talking to my daughter from thousands of miles away has been more emotional than I thought. Also, my arm hurts. If there were a way to get a quick ride to the hotel right now I would definitely take it, but there isn't, so I press on.

The thought comes suddenly, out of nowhere: I never opened the envelope that Nate gave me in Burgos! I haven't seen him since then, and there's a good chance he's wondering why I haven't reached out to let him know of my reaction.

The good news is, I get a jolt of energy. I need to get to the hotel and read the letter as quickly as possible. I find it shoved in the bottom of my suitcase and pull it out. Maybe it's some weird influence of the Camino, but I can hardly remember Nate, or maybe I don't want to remember him. I do recall that in Burgos he seemed very emotional.

Holding the letter in my hands, I realize I'm still not looking forward to reading it. The urgency is due more to my guilt about not having done it sooner. Anyway, I tear the envelope open.

What I find makes this truly one of the most surprising, or shocking, or incomprehensible moments of my life.

There's no letter, not even a note. There's only a check made out to me for twenty-five thousand dollars!

Chapter Forty

———◦◦◇◦◦———

Today, after walking for a bit with Natalie, we stop to have our credentials stamped, then for an iced tea at a roadside café.

I'm still in shock about the check from Nate and I don't know what I am going to do about it. It just seems really crazy. Should I seek him out to talk about it, or should I just ignore it, as if Nate had gone crazy and started wearing an aluminum foil hat on his head?

One thing I'm sure of: I'm not going to bring it up with Natalie.

My phone beeps and I apologize to her for having to look at it. What if it's Nate? In that case, I won't answer. But I always need to be prepared for something urgent from the kids.

There's a text but it's not from the kids. It's from Michael!

Michael and I began corresponding again a few years after my divorce. He is still married, but unhappily, and he admits to having several affairs over the years. After learning about this, I made it clear I would not be added to the list of his "other women," but I really did want to have a platonic friendship. We have succeeded in doing just this.

On this particular morning Michael texts me that while on vacation with his wife, his lover had broken off their three-year affair. He is heartbroken. I make the mistake of telling Natalie about this and she, being the all- knowing, wisewoman that she is, immediately launches into a very righteous "sermon" as to why I should not even be in touch with Michael! This, coming from a woman whose "walk of gratitude" is all about having her cake and eating it, too!

As we sit in this outdoor café, after a full morning of hiking about ten miles, she's lecturing me on exactly what I should say to Michael. But one should never argue with a narcissist. It's useless. You simply can't reason with an unreasonable person. So I just sit there, nodding in agreement. Then I sent a text back to Michael with my feelings in response to his message.

I'm sorry for his heartbreak. I'm sorry he's unhappy in his marriage. I understand his wanting to find love. But it's my humble opinion that as long as he stays married, he will not find the love of his life.

I share with him my belief that the Universe will not reward deceitful behavior. Does he really believe he will find true and lasting love while stepping out on his wife?

Chapter Forty-One

———◦◦◇◦◦———

"No amount of regret changes the past. No amount of anxiety changes the future. But any amount of Gratitude changes the present."

~Author Unknown

After our talk, Natalie and I split up. I walk ahead and she apparently catches a cab or calls one of our guides to get her, because by the time I arrive at the next hotel she is all freshened up and sitting under an umbrella, looking very stylish. She is wearing a lovely sun dress with a big floppy hat, and in front of her is – surprise – an open bottle of wine.

The hotel is on a remote route in Herrerias, a tiny town in a valley along a steep-sided and heavily-wooded pine and chestnut forest. This particular afternoon is picture perfect. The temperature is around seventy degrees. The sun is reflecting off the river below, with cows grazing in the fields between the hotel and the river. A breeze is lightly blowing, causing that soothing sound of wind rustling through the leaves of the trees.

I sit down next to Natalie, at her invitation, and so here we are again – me in my sweaty hiking clothes and she in her designer sunglasses and big, shiny earrings. She proudly tells me she is on her second bottle of wine and offers me a glass. Why not, I think, and we sit at the table for about forty-five minutes, relaxing and enjoying the beautiful scenery and wine.

Chapter Forty-Two

———◦◦◇◦◦———

I'm up at five and at breakfast earlier than the others. Today's hike is 22.5 kilometers, beginning with a steep climb in the morning. I have several cups of coffee before Natalie and Charlotte arrive. They enter the dining room together, sit at the other end of the table, obviously not interested in being polite. I'm used to this by now. By this point, Natalie and Charlotte have become a duo. Natalie rarely walks after lunch and Charlotte never misses a kilometer, but at the end of each walking day Natalie is waiting for Charlotte. Clearly she has also poisoned the well because any friendliness Charlotte once offered me has evaporated. I have become "persona non grata" to both. I order one more cup of coffee before going up to get my bags out of the room.

Coming back down the stairs, I overhear Natalie telling Charlotte how she *must* get away from me, and that she's *so* tired of me. Actually, I believe she timed this little speech so I would hear it. I knew I shouldn't let it bother me, but it does, so I quickly grab my backpack and leave before the others.

It's a lovely morning, but I realize that in my rush to get started I forgot to put my hat, mittens, and an additional down jacket into my pack. No matter, I keep going. I begin walking fast, and climbing. There's an eight-hundred-meter climb in front of me, and I'm trying to walk off my frustration, anger, and hurt feelings. Although I understand that Natalie has a "character disturbance" and I need to let what she says and does roll off by back, it still hurts. This is the essential, problematic dynamic between us: *She* is the "energy vampire"; *I* am the empath. She thrives on baiting me, manipulating me, and being all-around mean. Because I feel so damn much, it *does* hurt! I do try to do what is taught in many spiritual texts: do not take anything personally. Intellectually, I understand this dynamic. Unfortunately, my heart has not yet gotten the memo.

I'm passing pilgrims on the steep climb up, recognizing many of them. Each one greets me warmly. "*Buen Camino*," they say, and a few add that I'm "flying" up the mountain. And that's true, partly because it's gotten very cold, very fast. Without my clothing reinforcements, I hope to stay warm by almost running up this rugged terraine.

I make it to the top of the mountian in just over two hours – exhausted, dizzy, out of breath, and freezing! I am also looking around for Adam and the van.

After about ten minutes I see Brutis approaching. Adam gives me some nuts and water and asks how I managed to beat him to the summit. I tell him that I almost ran up the mountain, but now I'm not feeling too well. He offers me some juice and fruit, but I think the water and nuts are enough.

When I ask how far it is to the end of today's hike, he says it's another sixteen kilometers, but all flat and beautiful. Although he knows I'm not feeling well, Adam points out that I'll be missing a gorgeous part of the Camino if I stop now. So I relent and start off again, alone.

Adam was right. The scenery is gorgeous, and mostly flat. But the day is getting warmer. In fact, it's hot, with the temperature most likely in the eighties.

I am just outside of O'Cebreiro, a small but significant village along the Camino. O'Cebreiro is where Iglesia de Santa Maria Real, the oldest church associated with the pilgrim way, is located. Named for Santa Maria la Real, the patroness of this area, it also marks the final resting place of Don Elias Valina Sampedro (1929-1989), the parish priest who did so much during his lifetime to restore and preserve the integrity of the Camino. His efforts, including his idea to mark the route with the familiar yellow arrow, are in large part the reason we are able to walk it today.

As I walk along, enjoying the beautiful views, I question if I am on the correct path, but reason I must be following the map. I have no idea that I've "chosen" the alternate route, "Via Dragonte," which had been used by pilgrims of yore to traverse the Valcarce Valley. All I know is that I am totally alone.

Via Dragonte is remote and not well waymarked (in fact, there are virtually NO signs, though the books describe the markings as "obscure"), and I can definitely see why it would be desirable for those seeking a more contemplative way in the silence of nature. It is also much longer, adding another 8.2 kilometers to the already challenging, 26.3-kilometer climb. (I would later learn that pilgrims are warned to only take this route if they are "fit, have a good sense of orientation and an instinctive nature when faced with unexpected options." Certainly, no one would recommend it for someone nursing a significant wound!) I end up walking over 30 kilometers before finding my way to a small outdoor café. I am grateful on two counts – I have run out of water long ago and am incredibly thirsty, and I finally have cell service. I sit down and immediately call Adam to tell him I've gone off course. Fortunately, he's familiar with the Dragonte Route and he's going to come and get me, but it will take him at least thirty minutes.

In the meantime, I wait outside this isolated and delapidated bar, sitting in an old plastic chair that's literally on its last legs. The longer I wait, the worse I feel. I climbed so fast this morning and I've had nothing to eat except a few nuts. Eight hundred meters straight uphill in a bit over two hours, then a thirty minute rest before walking another twenty-four miles. I console myself with the fact that at least it was the scenic route!

Chapter Forty-Three

Adam and I get to our originally planned meeting place – a bar – to find the others waiting for us. They had all finished a while ago (having taken the correct route, they had saved themselves the extra 12 kilometers) and had been enjoying the sun and drinks. Now, they all climb into the van and off we go to the next hotel. I'm sitting between Adam, who is driving, and Charles. The girls are in the back. As we head out, I start to feel really sick and I know I'm going to pass out.

I've had a history of passing out from the time I was a child. I always have about a five to ten-second window before I lose consciousness., and that window is now. I tell Adam, "Please pull over. I'm sick."

When he does pull over, I get out and faint right there on the road. Adam sends the girls to get some ice, and what I recall is somebody lifts my head and tells me to drink from a bottle. It's a Coke, I think. The girls put ice on my neck and after about ten minutes, Adam asks if I can stand up. And I do, but I am far from steady!

We all get back into the van. This time, I am lying down in the back seat, still very out of it, not really comprehending where we are or what is being said. We arrive at the hotel. By now it's about seven p.m. I'm still weak, confused, and generally pretty damn sick! Someone takes me and my bags to my room and leaves me there, alone. Now freezing and exhausted, it takes everything I have to get out of my sweaty clothes and cover myself with a blanket.

It's dark when I wake up. I am extemely weak as well as thirsty, hungry, and dirty! I try calling down to the front desk, but I reach someone who doesn't speak English. I text Adam, and he has some water and a small plate of cheese sent to the room. I eat a few pieces of cheese, drink all the water, and climb back into bed.

Chapter Forty-Four

———◦◦◇◇◦◦———

cour~age, noun:
When resolve grows stronger than fear.

I didn't think I could feel any worse than I did when I crawled into bed on Saturday evening. By the time I wake up on Sunday afternoon, however, I realize how wrong I was. I feel even more wretched, and when I finally look at the antibiotic bottle the name is nothing I've ever heard of. This is when I understand that I must have had some sort of allergic reaction to this strange medicine. The combination of this and the dehydration is the cause of my current condition.

I text Adam and Stella. They're miles away with the rest of the group and suggest calling an ambulance to transport me to the nearest hospital. I really don't want to do that but I know I need help.

This is a large and modern hotel located in Sarria Centro, and I think maybe there's an in-house physician or a nurse who can give me an IV. But no such luck. Adam and Stella won't be back with the van before evening.

I don't know how, but I manage to get dressed and walk downstairs to the lobby. It's huge, busy with tourists and pilgrims. At the far end of the lobby I notice a restaurant. I walk over and ask the hostess if I can order something, but she shakes her head. It's too close to four p.m., when they close until reopening at nine for dinner. Could I just get a salad, nothing had to be cooked? She said no.

I actually begin to cry! I am so weak and thirsty! I am feeling powerless and vulnerable. But for a few small pieces of cheese, I haven't had anything to eat since Friday night, and in that time I've walked over fifty kilometers, climbed up a 2400-foot mountain, and fainted due to dehydration and the damn antibiotic!

Now the hostess takes pity on me. She says she'll bring me a salad and some water. She shows me where I can wait outside.

It's a warm and sunny late afternoon, and I sit at a table on the outdoor terrace. When a waiter comes over with water and a roll, I don't think I've ever been happier in my life. And then comes the salad, with fresh grilled chicken on top. I'm in heaven. This is the best meal of my life. By the time I finish my meal, I begin to come back to life. I sit on the terrace soaking in the sun while I watch people come and go.

A little later, as I'm waiting for the check, I see Natalie crossing the bridge over the river and entering the hotel. Obviously, she had not walked with the group that day since she's wearing nice clothes, sandals, and carrying two shopping bags.

She had stayed behind, probably slept late, then went into the city for a day of shopping and sightseeing. Despite my understanding of who and what she is I'm still surprised that Natalie hadn't bothered to check in on me before leaving. Neither had Adam or Stella, for that matter. I suppose no one knew how really sick I was. Afterall, I had not complained or reached out until this afternoon, and when they suggested I go to the hospital I declined. So maybe it was my fault. I have always been an excellent actress, especially when it means I can avoid being a nuisance.

"A damned nuisance!" – this is what I was called while growing up whenever I disturbed the natural routine of things, including being sick or hurt. I can trace my need to not make waves back to my childhood – even to a specific word used in my childhood – yet I could not understand why I was hurt and surprised that Natalie had taken the day off and never even attempted to see how I was. Why was this?

With a sigh I resign myself to the fact that I will never know exactly why people like Natalie do anything they do. Then I pay my bill, go upstairs, get my things in order for tomorrow, and go back to bed.

Chapter Forty-Five

———◦◇◇◦———

The following morning I am packed and ready to go for our seven a.m. breakfast meeting, which is miraculous given how awful I felt over the weekend. Today, we're supposed to walk 27.4 kilometers, from Sarria to Portomarin, and to be honest I'm not sure I'll be able to make it. Maybe, I think, I'll walk halfway, then ride the van to the next hotel. But as I walk, the landscape becomes more and more beautiful and I become more and more energized.

The day began cloudy with light rain, but by ten a.m., when I arrive at a bar to get a cup of coffee, it has stopped. By the time I leave the bar, the sun is beginning to shine. Once again I walk alone for the entire day, and with each passing kilometer I feel happier than I have since beginning the pilgrimage. The landscape is ever-changing along the Camino, but today it seems even more so. I walk past the church of Santa Marina with its somber medieval murals. From there I passed the ruins of the Sarria castle, which was destroyed during the uprising of the peasantry in the fifteenth century.

I head past a cemetery and then cross the Ponte Aspera – the "Rough Bridge" – which describes its coarsely cut stone. After passing gardens and statues, farmhouses and chapels, winding my way along woodland paths and chestnut groves, the land turns green with narrow lanes of granite stepping-stones raised above flood levels. From there, I pass a sign indicating it's just one hundred kilometers to Santiago!

Then I begin my descent into the Rio Mino valley.

I walk down a steep stairway, part of the original medieval bridge across the river Mino toward Portomarin. This is a lovely small town across the river and up another steep staircase, where I walk for just a block or two before coming to our inn. It is brand new, having just opened this year and is perfectly situated with views of the river.

Portomarin is a town built on a hill. The streets are cobblestone with shops and cafés leading to the central square, the Praza Conde de Fenosa. Overlooking it all is the Romanesque fortress-church of St. John. It was rebuilt from its original site, which is now submerged under waters of the Balesar reservoir. The church, with its breathtakingly beautiful prominent rose window, is ascribed to the workshop of Master Mateo, who carved the Portico da Gloria in Santiago.

Then something amazing happens. I see a man up ahead, and even from the back I know it's Nate. I had pretty much given up on seeing him again. Or maybe I'd just hoped I wouldn't see him. It occurred to me that he might be hiding, or maybe he had dropped out of the pilgrimage altogether. But there he is. It's Nate all right. No doubt about it.

For some reason, I feel a sudden surge of energy. Maybe he's been hiding, but I'm not going to hide. I quicken my pace and come up beside him.

"Hi, Nate."

He seems glad to see me. I would have expected some hesitancy, but there is nothing of the sort.

"Serena!" he says. "I'm so glad to see you. How have you been?"

I sense he wants to break stride in order to hug me, but I just keep walking.

I've noticed that sometimes, when people have done something they really feel embarrassed about, they just act like it never happened. It's like they forgot all about it, and they vibe that everybody else should forget about it too. Then again, maybe there are times when they really have forgotten about it.

I think it's nice of him to inquire how I've been, however, I don't see any reason to bring up the problem with my arm. Instead, I begin what could almost look like a casual conversation.

"I'm doing well, Nate. Just keeping on the path."

He looks pleased. "That's great. Me too. Staying the course."

"Nate, I'm glad I ran into you this afternoon. I want to speak with you about the envelope you gave me in Burgos."

He smiles, maybe a bit sheepishly. "Oh yeah, the envelope…"

"What were you thinking, Nate? What were you trying to do there?"

Now he looks more serious. "Well, what did you think I was trying to do?"

"I think you were trying to buy me. What else could I think? What would anyone think?"

We walk in silence for a moment. I can tell he's deep in thought.

Finally he says, "No, I was not trying to buy you. I was trying to express in pecuniary terms the emotional impact you've had on me – as, for example, if there's a sudden piece of good economic news, the stock market goes substantially up."

"The stock market?"

"I know that's a vulgar analogy, but I think you know what I mean."

He hesitates, then says, "Did it seem like an insignificant amount of money to you? I definitely could have cut a bigger check, and if I had, maybe the symbolism would have been more impactful. I'm also aware that emotions may not be entirely fungible. Feelings, especially erotic feelings, might not be translatable into another form, like money. Do you understand what I'm trying to say?"

I take a deep breath. "I'm not really sure that I do."

"What does it sound like?"

"Well, it sounds like you were attracted to me, and you tried to express it with a check."

"And that was a failure?"

"Yes."

Suddenly he stops walking and takes hold of my arm so that I have to stop and face him. Thank God it's my good arm.

"Then let me express my feelings for you in a far superior way, Serena. There's no one else around. Let's go over there where we have some privacy."

I literally can't believe what I'm hearing. I feel physically ill, severely nauseated. Speech is impossible, but I manage to pull my arm away and take a step backward. I must have gone completely pale, because Nate looks increasingly concerned.

"Serena..." he says.

I'm starting to walk ahead. If he tries to follow, I'll run. Even weak, I'm sure I can outrun him.

I can hear calling out behind me. "Serena, just tear up that check! Write 'void' on it!"

Oh my God. Oh my God.

I arrive at our hotel shortly thereafter. It's beautiful, simple and elegant, my room looking out on the river. I lock the door and collapse on the bed! Grateful I am alone!

Chapter Forty-Six

———◦◦◇◇◦◦———

The next morning we walk from the hotel in Portomarin across the river and out of the town. It's clear and cool as we get started around seventy-thirty. The surrounding countryside is a lush green. It's now the end of May, and in northern Spain the flowers are in full bloom with bright colors everywhere. I doubt that in all the years pilgrims had been finding their way along the Camino Frances, any had better weather.

By the end of the day, we arrive at a charming inn purchased by a married couple several years ago. It's obvious that they're intent on keeping this old manor home true to its history. The inn has been turned into a small, elegant, "off the beaten track" bed-and-breakfast with twelve rooms. When I meet the owner's mother, she speaks no English, but manages to communicate that she had made all the beautiful lace curtains on the windows of my room. She must have learned this craft from one of the real masters. I'm sure she is in her late eighties, yet she's still making her remarkable creations.

Because I have very little room in my suitcase, I have not purchased anything along the Camino. But when I see this woman's work, I ask her if she has any items for sale. She does, but not many. I buy a few of her hand towels, one for me and several for family members. I make a point of telling her that her towels were the only things I had bought during my seven-week pilgrimage. It makes her very happy.

The couple who owns this inn have created a totally self-sufficient "farm to table" property. They grow their own fruits and vegetables. They raise their own livestock. Everything on the table is cooked or baked by them. I have no idea how the three of them managed such a big operation. They of course have some help, but I'm told that for the most part it all is done by the owners. Amazing.

Chapter Forty-Seven

So far, I've taken over four thousand photographs on the Camino. It did not take me long to realize that journaling at the end of every day would be too much to ask! I was too tired to write, so instead I decided to create a "photo jour-nal." I've chosen music to accompany the photos of each day and my song for today is "Hold On," by Wilson Phillips. This turns out to be very apropos, for holding on is precisely what I will do for the next two days, until we arrive in Santiago.

Today begins as another beautiful spring day along the Camino. There's a natural canopy of trees above our heads, with lush green fields, forests, old stone bridges, farmland, and vineyards. I stop for an iced tea around noon. By now the day is hot, and I'm a sweaty, thirsty mess.

Because we're now less than a hundred kilometers from Santiago, the number of pilgrims has exponentially increased. Most of these people are walking with the original intention of the pilgrims from centuries past: absolution of sin.

This tradition goes back to 813 A.D., when a shepherd named Pelayo was drawn to a field in Libredon by a "bright light" or "star." This is where we get Santiago de Compostela – from the Latin word for field – *compus* – and the *stellae*, or stars, of Saint James (aka Sant Iago).

St. James became the patron saint of Spain, and the first written record of pilgrimage to Santiago was between 950 -1072. Between the twelfth and fourteenth centuries, Santiago de Compostela grew in prestige. Tens of thousands of pilgrims chose to suffer the hazards of this route every year during the Middle Ages. A combination of the relative accessibility of the route and the miracles associated with the relics of the Saint beneath the cathedral were contributing factors in its popularity. The "Camino de Santiago" was firmly established, with the image of St. James the Pilgrim – "Santiago Peregrino" – portrayed all along the route with staff, Bible, wide brim hat, and scallop shell, or "concha." The concha survives as the single identifying symbol of the pilgrim to Santiago. Under Pope Calixtus II, the first travel guide to the Camino was created, dividing it into thirteen stages beginning in St. Jean Pied de Port.

For many, the Knights Templar became a cornerstone of this heritage of the Camino. With the rising influence of the Knights, they became a threat to the Papacy. As a result, on Friday, October 13, 1314, the majority of the Knights Templar were arrested and put to death. The legacy of this massacre lives on, which is why Friday 13th is considered unlucky today.

Today, many who walk the last hundred kilometers do so as a religious "sacrifice." Most of my fellow travelers have looked to be in good physical condition, but that's changing as we get closer to the end, with many overweight pilgrims. These are not typical hikers. Many are walking in large church groups, not properly dressed for such rugged terrain. In order to be considered "official" a pilgrim has to complete the last hundred kilometers, which should only take three or four days. But for those who are older and heavier, it takes up to a week!

Today, in order to stay two consecutive nights in the delightful inn, the guides shuttle us from our last checkpoint to the Pazo Santa Maria. It's during this short drive that Natalie chooses to hurl her cruel – and, I decide, FINAL – judgement at me. By itself, what she says might not seem so significant, but it really is the last straw.

"Tender Ladies," which I had previously chosen as my song of the day, is playing on the radio and I say it's one of my favorites. I'm really glad to hear it at this point – quite moved, in fact – and for some reason this really sets Natalie off. She's terribly offended by my response to what she calls "sentimental bullshit." She puts on a tremendous performance. It's all I can do to keep from jumping out of the van, or hitting Natalie in the face with a plastic water bottle.

Instead, I just sit there, silently reminding myself to, for the last time, act with dignity and keep calm. But I know what I'm going to do. By the time I walk into my room, I know I will finish the Camino, but unless absolutely necessary I will not spend one more moment near that wicked bitch Natalie! It takes several hours for me to call the States and wait for confirmation that I did have a seat on a flight out of Santiago on Friday evening. I would fly into Madrid and stay at the airport hotel there before taking an 8 a.m. flight back to JFK. This last-minute change cost me over three thousand dollars, but at this point I would have paid anything.

After jotting down the details, I call Kelly and ask her to cancel my three nights in the hotel in Santiago. I was calling her on Wednesday, giving her forty-eight hours' notice in hopes my hotel costs would be credited back to me. She said she would try, but the hotel never did give me a refund.

After speaking to Kelly, I know I have to tell Adam and Stella that I will be leaving Santiago Friday evening. This means I will not be able to attend the Pilgrim's Mass or the farewell dinner. I will also miss the guided tour of the Cathedral on Saturday morning. To top it all off, while I was in Madrid with Evelyn prior to the Camino I had purchased a really pretty red dress. I had carried this with me *all* across Spain, intending to wear it in Santiago one of the nights I was there.

As it turns out I don't need to contact Adam or Stella, because Kelly beats me to it. Adam comes to my room with an alarmed look on his face and asks me what happened. I realize that though he had been in the van he might not have heard the entire exchange from up front. By this time a few hours have passed so I'm calm and composed when I tell him something unexpected came up at home that necessitated my early return.

He stands there and stares at me, first in confusion and then with scrutiny. He is not swallowing this and suggests we take a walk. As we're strolling the large and beautiful grounds, we slow to a stop and turn toward each other.

"Serera, *what really happened?*"

"Adam, I need you to promise that you and Stella will keep this between the three of us."

He replies, "Of course."

I take a deep breath, not quite sure where to begin or what to say.

"Adam, you and Stella have been wonderful. You both have been terrific guides and you were so helpful when I fell, and when I had to go back to the hospital, and when you took me to another doctor when my arm became infected for the second time. Plus, the TLC you gave me when I passed out. I never imagined any of this would have happened. I'm embarrassed but at the same time I feel so fortunate to have had you and Stella beside me this past month."

"Well, thank you for your kind words…"

"But," I continue, "the interpersonal dynamics of our group has been a challenge. Would you agree about that?"

"Serena, Stella and I have discussed this countless times. We have watched this whole thing play out and we hated it. But we didn't really know how to intervene, or how to help."

"Well, it wasn't your responsibility to help. Natalie and Charlotte have behaved like teenage girls, but we're all adults. I've done my best to not bow to their level. I also tried to downplay it, hoping you and Stella, as well as Charles would not be affected. Now, I see that didn't work,"

Adam is shaking his head. "I am so sorry that you are leaving us as soon as we get into Santiago. You'll miss all the festivities. You're not going to celebrate your success. You won't even have a chance to see any of Santiago. But I'm proud of you. You didn't let any of this stop you. You never gave up."

" I made up my mind, long ago, to never let anything or anyone stop me from finishing this Camino. But as soon as I walk into Santiago, I plan to fly out within the hour."

Adam and I hug as our conversation comes to an end. We know that if Natalie discovers my plan to make an early exit, she will definitely make a scene. She has already created too much drama on this "spiritual pilgrimage" of ours!

Chapter Forty-Eight

———◦◦◇◇◦◦———

"He who blames others has a long way to go on his journey. He who blames himself is halfway there. He who blames no one has arrived."

~Author Unknown

That night I have a strange dream that makes it impossible to get back to sleep. I write it down in the hopes of understanding any messages it holds.

I'm five or six years old, in the back seat of my father's car. He's driving with my mother next to him in the front seat. Somehow, even in the dream, I realize we have gone back in time.

I say, "We've gone back in time!"

They nod in agreement. I ask them how they feel, since they both look young and healthy. But my mother says, "I'm feeling a little tired."

That's odd, because she never says she's tired. But perhaps she's tired because she has several young children at home. My dad, on the other hand, says, "I feel great!"

Dad parks the car and my mother gets out. Then he turns around to me in the backseat and says, "Serena, take a look at this."

I scoot up and peer over into the front seat to see a small gift bag next to my father. It's filled with sample-size bottles of the cologne he used to wear. I jump over the seat to get a better look, and then I throw my arms around his neck and begin to cry. For some reason he says, "Baby, time is going by so fast."

The dream is so real to me. I can feel my own innocence, and that I am small and safe, knowing my father will always be there for me. I feel his love and his affection. And he had called me "Baby," his pet name for me ever since I could remember. I had rarely thought about it in the decade since he'd died, and hearing it again, even in a dream, brought the emotions steamrolling through me.

While all of this is happening, my mother has walked around the front of the car and is peering into my father's window. Neither Daddy nor I say anything, but we do not open his door.

So my mother is standing outside the car while I'm hugging my dad and crying – sobbing, really. After he tells me that time is going by so fast, I cry out, "No! Time has not gone by fast, not at all! *NOTHING* has been the same since you left."

That's when I wake up. I'm crying so hard that I'm afraid of waking whoever is in the next room. As I lie there, I somehow have access to those long-ago feelings I experienced as a young child. I am actually *feeling and sensing* precisely how I viewed the world from the perspective of a child! I felt loved, protected, and safe when I was with my dad! I felt accepted and I felt like he approved of me. I felt his unconditional love for me; this, in stark contrast to how I have felt as an adult, which is alone, unloved, unseen, unheard and unsafe! I have felt vulnerable and

I have grieved the absence of someone who could protect me. It sounds so childish, but perhaps this dream was meant to remind me of who I really am!?

Though it's still dark, I get out of bed and walk the fifty yards to the patio. Because of the full moon, I can see my way to the clothesline hanging there. My clothes are dry, so I take them back to my room, get showered and packed, and show up for our second-to-last morning meeting.

As the meeting ends, Stella asks me to join her. She wants my help with something before leaving the hotel. We get into a waiting cab and she tells me that Adam has filled her in about my plans. She assures me she understands my choice to leave early. Then she asks what, if anything, I feel I've learned from this experience.

After a long moment in thought, I tell her that I realize how important kindness is, and I believe it's actually easier to be kind than unkind. I assure her that she and Adam have been wonderful guides.

Chapter Forty-Nine

———∘◇◇◇∘———

The song of the day is Chris Botti's rendition of "Time to Say Goodbye" – a fitting choice as we near the end of the journey.

I start out around eight a.m., and before noon I've arrived at Vivienne's "bar," which is just thirty-three kilometers outside of Santiago. She has been working on this property for the last ten years, converting two ancient structures into a café and home.

As I approach this charming piece of land, I see the signs that have been made for all to see as they walk the last few kilometers. One sign says, "Welcome to Tabernavella." This is the name of the bar. The Spanish word "taberna" means inn or tavern, and "vella" means beautiful, or "super cool," "rad," and all-around nice.

Actually, it pretty perfectly describes the property and what the property expresses to all pilgrims. As I walk toward the newly opened and renovated bar there are more handmade signs nailed to trees: "WELCOME!" "ALL RELIGIONS!" "ALL BELIEFS!" "ALL SEXES!" "ALL CULTURES!" "ALL AGES!" "ALL SIZES!" "ALL COLORS!" "ALL PEOPLE!" This describes Vivienne's intention for creating this retreat.

The bar is finished, but the structure that will eventually become her home is still far from completion. Both buildings are being restored to their original, historic identity, with red tile roofs. The sides of each building consist of the original stones. Those that could be cleaned remain, the others have been replaced.

When I see Vivienne, we hug and she begins to take me on a tour of her Camino taberna. She remembers my appreciation of beauty and design. She asks me what she can do with her large outdoor patio. It is simple white concrete and stands in stark contrast to the deep red and earth tones of the restored café. I suggest large outdoor sisal rugs. They're rugged and inexpensive, would last a season, and could be replaced each year. Vivienne asks if I know where she can find these and I give her the names of several different websites where I know she will find exactly what will work here. She thanks me and agrees the idea of outdoor rugs is a perfect solution. We continue the tour of both the inn and her home.

Vivienne explains why this project has taken so long. Apparently, and not surprising to me, the "red tape" involved with any new construction along the Camino, an historic and protected land, requires excessive patience. It also requires anyone who begins something like this to get up to speed on the Spanish culture of "hurry up and wait." She purchased the property from a family that had owned it for generations, and in Spain, everyone on the deed must agree to the sale. In this case, as Vivienne explains, with each successive generation, there were more heirs due to the addition of spouses. This resulted in as many as thirty to forty individuals having their say in the sale of this property! Added to this was the frustration of dealing with government agents in Santiago, the endless historic regulations

---

of the Camino, and various architects and contractors. No wonder it has taken her over ten years to get this far. I admire her patience and tenacity to see this project through. It's obvious she has succeeded in fulfilling her original mission of providing a tranquil retreat for any pilgrim who needs a rest and a cold drink.

I end this day back at the peaceful inn located in Arzua. Tonight is the last night on the Camino. I shower and grab a salad and glass of wine from the dining room before heading to bed. It's still light outside.

Chapter Fifty

I wake when it's still dark outside, but the moon is shining bright in the clear sky. I watch the sunrise over the vineyards behind our inn, another warm and sunny spring morning. After our final breakfast meeting, I began walking this final stage of the Camino.

The dense and ever-present eucalyptus trees provide shade and peace. As I near the city of Santiago, busloads of pilgrims appear on the road. After eleven kilometers I arrive at our designated picnic spot at Monte del Gozo, an elevated site overlooking the city of Santiago.

Adam and Stella have provided us with our last picnic lunch – a welcome treat of handmade salads, fresh-baked bread, olives, iced tea, lemonade, and lots of water so we can replenish our supply and sweets for dessert.

As I enter Santiago, Adam is waiting for me. I'm the first in our small group to arrive. He walks me down some steps into the Praza Obradoiro, where men are lined up on each side of the stairwell, playing bagpipes. This is the welcome for each pilgrim, taking his or her final steps of the Camino.

I surprise myself by getting choked up as I descend the steps. I suppose everyone experiences different emotions, from euphoria to exhaustion upon seeing the Cathedral. I feel honored and grateful to have arrived safely into the noisy and crowded town square. Had I planned to stay for the weekend, as was my original intention, I think I would have returned to the square later, when it was less crowded and more quiet, in order to really take in the scenery.

Because I won't be able to take the official tour of the cathedral, I know I have a few minutes before the others arrive. So, I quickly walk myself through. The cathedral interior is undergoing a renovation, due for completion in 2021. I pass through Master Mateo's Portico de Gloria, or Door of Glory. The inner portico was carved between 1166 and 1188, with the exterior facade added in 1750. The central column has Christ in Glory flanked by the apostles and, directly underneath, St. James is represented as intercessor between Christ and the pilgrim.

Over the centuries millions of pilgrims have worn finger holes in the solid marble in gratitude for their safe arrival.

I proceed to the high altar, climbing the stairs and hugging a sculpture of the Apostle. This is a tradition for each pilgrim upon completion of their Camino. I say a prayer of thanks for the opportunity to experience this once in a lifetime adventure.

Unfortunately, because of the construction and my abbreviated visit, I'm not able to witness the swinging of the giant incense burner, called Botafumeiro. This was originally used to fumigate sweaty and possibly disease-ridden pilgrims. The ritual requires a half dozen attendants, called tiraboleiros. In recent years this has become so popular that the seating capacity was expanded from seven hundred to a thousand!

As I return to the square outside, Adam is holding a bottle of champagne anticipating the arrival of the rest of our group. When the others arrive he makes a toast to our completion of our Camino. Then we head over to the Pilgrims Office.

The office has tight security as well as a long line of tired pilgrims. We are a small group led by our Spanish guides, making our wait shorter before handing over our stamped *credencials*. I've carefully gone through mine to be sure that each day along the Camino Frances had been stamped at least twice, with the correct date and place. Once we've all done this, Adam takes our credencials to the team of "amigos," where he leaves them for certification as bona fide pilgrims. Because I'm leaving soon, Stella promises to mail my *certificado* to me; the others will get theirs back in the next day or two. We discuss this stealthfully as I don't want anyone to know I'm leaving early.

Chapter Fifty-One

———◦◦◇◦◦———

We enter the grand hotel and the others go to their rooms to shower and dress for the formal dinner that evening. I find a ladies room off the lobby and take off the running shoes I wore across Spain. Without any sentimentality I proceed to throw them in the garbage can. I also remove my worn-out and sweaty top and throw that away as well. I do my best to wash my arms and torso with a paper towel, change into a clean t-shirt and sandals, and go back to the lobby. I ask the concierge to call a taxi and I wait for it to arrive.

Breathing a sigh of relief, realizing I've been able to escape notice by Natalie and Charlotte, Charles appears in front of me and says, "Serena, did I hear that you are leaving us now?"

I glance around, making sure it's only Charles with no one else within earshot. "Yes, that's right," I tell him. "Something came up and I have to leave this evening."

Charles has kept mostly to himself over the course of our thirty-five days on the road, but it did not escape my notice that he regularly checked up on each woman in the group. I had not spent much time with him, but I always found him to be pleasant as well as a true gentleman.

Charles tells me he was sorry I would be missing the dinner tonight, the Pilgrim Mass tomorrow, as well as the cathedral tour, not to mention a weekend RELAXING and shopping in Santiago.

I thank him for his company and then he does something that surprises me. He hugs me and says, "Serena, I really admired the fact that you continued this pilgrimage after your accident. If I had an injury like yours, I know I would have gone home. But you stuck it out even with a second infection. I'm just really impressed that you never gave up after the other challenges you endured along the way."

He was obviously referring to the sophomoric behavior of Natalie and Charlotte. I told him I appreciated his compliments and admitted to feeling relief upon my completion of the journey. I added that I had tried to keep the dysfunctional situation between the two women and myself quiet, as I did not want to create any more drama than they had done themselves.

"Ah, yes," he says with a smile. "The two girls, although from my perspective, it was Natalie who undermined the spiritual quality of this whole enterprise. Her indiscretions have been indiscreet, to put it mildly."

I'm not sure exactly what he's referring to. Natalie can't shut up, is that what he means?

Charles notices my puzzled look. "Uh-oh, have I let a cat out of a bag? I mean, every time I saw her, Natalie had another story about her interludes with that man named Nate! His financial generosity. His sexual generosity, if that's the right word. She used very different vocabulary, of course."

"Nate? You said Nate?"

"Yea, do you know him?" Charles looks concerned. He continues, "I've never met him. Just heard a lot about him from Natalie."

Later, I will flash back on the little things – how Nate ignored Natalie that day he introduced himself at the café, and how she, who talked so freely about her exploits, never mentioned Nate to me. But in that moment, as had happened so many other times whenever Natalie was involved, I am speechless.

"No, I don't know anyone named Nate. And I don't know Natalie either, not really. Thank you for your friendship, Charles."

My cab is pulling up to the hotel. I give Charles a quick hug. As the driver comes around to help with my bags, I jump into the back seat of the cab.

Chapter Fifty-Two

---◦◦◦◦◦---

I'm trying not to think. If I do think, I might go crazy. I'll just keep my mind on getting out of here.

The drive to the Santiago airport takes only ten minutes. My flight is due to leave at nine p.m., so I have at least an hour before departure. I find a tiny food court in the airport and have a salad before boarding.

I have never traveled in this condition before... Dirty and sweaty, but I'll soon be able to shower in the airport hotel my travel agent had reserved for me in Madrid. Although I will only get about four hours of sleep, what I really need is to get clean!

I board the small prop plane on the tarmac and sit beside a young Spanish woman and her nine-year-old son. After takeoff, the boy is very chatty and asks me all sorts of questions. She tries to hush child but I assure her that I enjoy talking with her son.

He sees how I'm dressed and has noticed my enormous backpack. He asks if I had walked the Camino and I reply, "Yes, and I just finished about four hours ago!"

He has a look of surprise and asks if I did the full Camino. "Yes, I did."

His mother adds, "All Spaniards are in awe of the pilgrims who walk the entire five hundred fifty miles."

We chat easily and effortlessly the entire flight. She confides in me that she is divorced and a single mother. She and her son are going to Madrid for the weekend. She is meeting an old boyfriend there...for the first time in years. They will be staying with a mutual friend who has children the same age as her son. After we land and say "Good Bye", I catch sight of her and her son across the baggage claim area. A few minutes later, as I walk over to grab my bag I see her hugging a very good-looking man. I get my bags and, as I walk to the curb, she sees me and I give her thumbs up. I hope she finds love again. She deserves it. We all do.

I get into another cab and provide the name of the airport hotel my travel agent has reserved. I'm a bit surprised when fifteen minutes later we're still driving. I had assumed an "airport hotel" would be not far from the airport. It's another fifteen minutes before we pull into a very basic looking motel.

I get my bags and enter the lobby. Even after midnight, the place is packed, with lines to the check-in counter. I'm exhausted and just want to get to my room and take off the sweaty clothes that were my "uniform" for the past six weeks.

As I wait to check in, I think to myself that I'll be lucky to get just a few hours of sleep. It's after midnight now, and I have to get up by five in order to get back to the Madrid airport by seven. My flight is leaving shortly thereafter.

I finally make my way up to the front of the line. I give my name and credit card, and I expect a rapid exchange of information to obtain my key.

It doesn't work this way. The check-in woman tells me there's no room reserved for me!

I quickly show her my confirmation print-out, but she just repeats that there's no reservation. I ask her how that is even possible when I have proof of my reserved room.

She glances out at the crowd for a second, and then tells me that if I really want this room – *really want it* – it will cost me two thousand Euros!

I'm totally incredulous. "What! Why?"

Well, it turns out the following day is the final match between the Madrid soccer team and their big rival. People from all over the world have flown in for this weekend. That's the explanation I get from the woman behind the desk, who once again says that, yes, if I really want the room, I can have it for two thousand Euros.

No! Absolutely not! I ask her to call me a cab back to the Madrid airport.

Chapter Fifty-Three

In the cab I make a plan for getting to the American Airlines Admirals Club. There I'll be able to shower and change and get clean. I'll find a chair and wait until morning.

I'm back at the airport by three a.m., and the cab drops me off at the American Airlines terminal. I get my bags to one of the doors into the terminal, but it's locked! I go from one door to the next and they're all locked!

By now I've been awake for over twenty-four hours. I walked the last twenty kilometers of the Camino, flew from Santiago, took a cab thirty minutes out of Madrid, then another thirty-minute drive back to Madrid. Now all the doors to the airport are locked, and there's not a soul around.

I begin to cry. I can't think straight. I'm beyond tired. And I'm so dirty. How can I get into the damn airport?

As I stand there crying and feeling sorry for myself, I hear a car door. I turn and see a crew of pilots heading for one of the sets of doors that had been locked. I grab my bags and run toward them. One of the pilots sees me and waits, holding the door open for me. Is this a miracle or what?

He speaks Spanish. I speak English. Between us, I try to ask him about the American Airlines Admirals Club. But we can't understand each other, so I follow the pilots to a security entrance.

The man at security says I need to check my bags before passing through. I try to tell him that I want to find the Admirals Club – I show him my members card – but he shakes his head. I have to check my bags before going through security. By now the baggage check is closed.

Again, I start to cry, which does me absolutely no good. Plus, the pilots are long gone. It's just me and the security agent who wouldn't budge.

I have no choice. I start walking around the terminal, hoping to locate some sort of chair to recline in, or a few chairs without armrests where I can lie down.

Nothing. There are only molded plastic seats strung together by the dozens, all with armrests. There would be no lying down tonight. Slowly, I begin going through my bags to look for a clean sweatshirt, as with the air conditioning the place is about sixty degrees. I'm dressed in a sleeveless top with the leggings I had been wearing since the day before. I have dried sweat all over my body along with the red clay affixed to my feet and legs. I'm freezing, exhausted, and so angry! I swear at Natalie! I swear at Spain! I swear at everyone! I curse God for leading me to this fucking Camino!

Epilogue:
That was then. This is...What?

—◦◦◇◦◦—

"The butterfly does not look back at the caterpillar in shame, just as you should not look back at your past in shame. Your past was part of your own transformation."

~Author unknown

Several weeks later and back home, I receive a package from Stella with my credentials, along with a certificate for finishing the Camino. Stella includes a note:.

Dear Serena,

After over one month together, it was bittersweet saying good-bye. Sweet, because of the time shared and for everything that you brought to this group. Bitter, because we probably will not have this time again.

I want to thank you for your openness, kindness, and generosity. It was an absolute pleasure, and I hope that you returned home with fond memories to share with your family and friends.

I remember many things you said, but mostly that "it is easy to be kind. It is easier to be kind than unkind." Thank you for your own kindness and open spirit. I wish you all the best from here forward. Your path starts now.

Buen Camino!

Love,
Stella

I appreciate Stella's sentiments and one phrase in her letter really stands out: "Your path starts now."

My first thought is, "Wait a minute. I thought I just finished the path. Now there's a new path?"

So I need to make sense of this. Intuitively I believe Stella is right. From the Camino, I wanted completion. That was my focus. I wasn't really thinking about something new. I was yearning to get out from under everything that had gotten really old.

When I try to think specifically about what exactly it was that had become so old and burdensome, the answer could not be more obvious. It was everything that I experienced with those individuals throughout my life who saw me as having no intrinsic value or worth. What they did see was something they could use in order to accomplish their selfish desires. Perhaps some saw my light and tried to claim it as their own. Because many had TOLD me they loved me, I lived in a state of confusion much of the time! This confusion was created by their ACTIONS. They told me they loved me but they treated me in an Unloving way, without any compassion. This had become the common theme in my life. And I had tried to make sense of it for many years. Finally, I had put the pieces together and understood how I had unwittingly been their "puppet" while they were the "puppeteer". I was so ready to be done with the whole story! I was desperate to be rid of it, ALL of it, for once and for all!.

Now I have a sudden revelation. Maybe I *have* freed myself from it, but not in a way that I ever imagined.

I set out on the Camino with the hope that six weeks in nature and movement, along the oldest spiritual path in the world, would create the clarity and the new start that I needed. I did not give much thought to those I would meet along the Camino, but when I did, I *assumed* they would be mature, kind and evolved individuals. I expected my Camino to give me what I thought I wanted, which was the light to see me through the darkness of my past. I hoped my experiences along the Camino, as well as what I had learned up to that point would help me find the healing I had been searching for.

Amazingly, what I met was more of the same darkness I was trying to leave behind. It's funny, if I can remain objective about it. God sent me *more of what I was running from!* Even more amazingly, maybe this did help me to heal, because I *do* finally feel free! I had to let go of all of the confusion and pain. I had to REALLY love myself. So, I no longer beat myself up for not being the "perfect" soul others demanded of me. I feel liberated from my past and know that I can choose a future free from this darkness. I think about Natalie. I think about Nate. I think about that night in the Madrid airport when it all seemed to come crashing down.

But, I no longer waste my time or energy on the scared little boy who I once believed was my husband. Not anymore. I have learned to never, again, waste my time and energy on anyone who shows me their dark truth. As one who seeks to shine my light upon the truth, nobody who lives beneath the shadows in the darkness will be granted permission into my new story!

Is this what transformation means? If I – or any of us – are destined to keep experiencing the same thing over and over again, maybe the only answer is *not to* run away or try to avoid more of the same. But rather, to surrender to what WAS and vow to go forward loving ourselves the way we once loved them. To forgive the person we WERE and let go of those in our past with love. And finally, to realize that we all have it within us to choose a different *WAY*. We all are responsible for creating the life we want.

Is that my new path? Hmmm…

I realize that beginning in St. Jean Pied de Port, all the way to Santiago, I was getting messages from my fellow pilgrims as well as spirits on the other side, urging me to leave the darkness of my old story and to see the light of my *true* story!

So now, I begin anew. *MY* Camino, just as *my* life, taught me lessons I needed to learn, in order to return to *ME!* This is my new path. This is the Camino that never ends.

The End

Made in the USA
Middletown, DE
09 January 2022

58290963R00129